# UPON ARRIVAL

## PRELUDE

John T. Eber Sr.
MANAGING EDITOR

A publication of

Eber & Wein Publishing
Pennsylvania

Upon Arrival: Prelude


Library of Congress
Cataloging in Publication Data

ISBN 978-1-60880-661-4

Proudly manufactured in the United States of America by

Eber & Wein Publishing

Pennsylvania

# A Note from the Editor . . .

A little kingdom I possess
  Where thoughts and feelings dwell,
And very hard I find the task
  Of governing it well.

—Louisa May Alcott
*from* "My Kingdom"

Welcome, poets and readers, to our next beloved volume of poetry, where "the mind can weave itself warmly in the cocoon of its own thoughts and dwell a hermit anywhere" (in James Russell Lowell's words). This is a safe place to share your thoughts, announce your successes, and grieve your losses with kindred spirits. Approach these pages as a meditative act, one that requires your focus and patience but will bring you peace and enlightenment.

Poetry is made of the mind-stuff on which you dwell, the ideas that run circles in your head; writing—specifically poetry—allows you to release those nagging thoughts, whether positive or negative. Feeling down? Or maybe you're bursting with emotions: Get a small notebook—or just a single sheet of paper!—and start writing. Not only is journaling a great mental release and path to inner harmony, it's a warehouse for all your writing ideas. At any time you please, you can walk down the aisles of your past thoughts, selecting those that cry out for development. That's your next poem, and we can't wait to read the polished draft!

We lean on inspiration to fire our machines of creation, but seasoned writers know the necessity of discipline. Committed writing is a physical practice, one that requires exhaustive training, continuous dedication, reflecting on results, and staying abreast of emerging trends. Amateur writers can also benefit from even a small amount of discipline. Start by writing a little bit each day, maybe with your morning coffee.

Another easy way to improve your writing is to read more. You will absorb more than just plot; you'll become more familiar with proper grammar, capitalization and punctuation without even realizing it. You'll be exposed to different sentence structures and will surely find inspiration for your own work. As Samuel Taylor Coleridge wrote, "Advice is like snow; the softer it falls the longer it dwells upon and the deeper it sinks into the mind." So give your mind the chance to sink deeper.

While poetry writing can be a studious practice, it's also a spiritual practice with an intimate transaction between writer and reader, speaker and audience, and corporeal and ethereal, but firstly between writer and self. We think of writers as performers for an audience, but before the artist shows off her masterpiece, she first nurtures the seed within herself. Wrap yourself in creature comforts, get out your favorite pen and notepad, and start releasing your cocooned verse. Together, we go forward into our own "little kingdoms" of thought, and there we shall dwell until meeting again between the covers of a book.

Desiree Halkyer
Editor

## Saddle Up, Writers

A phrase that comes to you like lightning in a bottle
You can't grab a pencil and paper fast enough
Before it disappears like the end of a rainbow
It rolls in like an open range fire chasing wild horses
And buffalo racing each other neck and neck
Now you're off to the Races
Then it's as easy as lighting a match on worn chaps
So stick to your guns
Stay with the cattle drive to the end of the trail
To give yourself a chance of success
As a reward for all of those endless hours of
Writing and typing and rewriting some more
With deadlines looming like galloping horses
To the finish line, we can't forget the editing either
Until we're cross eyed at midnight
Ride that bronco until the last word is written
So always keep your saddle bags full of ideas
For the next one
If inspiration comes and lightning strikes your
Silver bottle, let the genie escape her shackles
Puts on your spurs on to ride a wild cyclone
Oh, we have to Love it! Don't we?

Zeke Castro
*Alamogordo, NM*

*I'm a retired sheet metal worker of fifty years and am currently writing the history of my hometown founded in 1898. I grew up in the 1940s, and I have recorded all the stories I can remember. I am also the author of the book* An Outlaw Called Kidd *about the reality of Billy the Kid, which my grandmother knew well. I'm a member of Western Writers of America and we have annual awards of western genre in which poetry is included. This is my first try at poetry; it took me thirty minutes to rough it out.*

## Free Hearts

Open unhidden
Blooming under their Son
Singing, smiling, unashamed
They do not fear
They will not be broken
They do not hide
They will not be bruised
They do not flinch
No anger strikes them
They will grow again, this day, in Love

Free hearts
So small, so gentle
With just a touch
They fall and die
Free hearts
So small, so loving
With your sweet love, they touch the sky

Chuck Worthy
*Gig Harbor, WA*

## Introduction

I asked them to give me a chance
Maybe even to notice me at first glance
Trying to hold a strong stance
Because I knew that I could advance
I said let me stand for who I am
Don't suffocate me with the stereotypes
That fall out of your mouth like all the other words
That you use to choke me with
Feeling naked as a blanket of confidence was stripped off me
Society's insecurities suddenly holding me within its arms

I was told that my male peers were stronger, smarter
And that I should take caution to be guarded, quiet
We teach our girls to prosper, but not too prosperous
We teach our girls to be strong, but not too strong
Because both of us know damn well that these may
Be a threat to the men around us
Apparently, my sole purpose here was to look pretty
And will always be
I want them to read my story and call me glory
And observe my move just to prove that I can Stand strong,
So why don't you all come along?
Around us, we notice signs of injustice
I am not his princess, but much rather my *own* ruler

They began mocking me
Just to lower my self-esteem
They looked for avoidance and incompetence
But when we came together and stood strong,
All they found was pure *confidence*

Shreya Hegde
*Plainsboro Center, NJ*

## Memories of Crushes

As I cleaned my room out of various memories,
Some good, some bad
A journal caught my eye
As I opened I discovered,
The crushes I had written about over the years
How I behaved towards them
What I learned
Why I realized I could never date them
One crush did catch my eye
One that I learned the hardest lessons from
Yet it's the only one I run into years later
For a moment I laughed at the entries
I was such a child then
So many emotions
So much to deal with
Then I realized something
I looked at that same crush then and looked at him now
The eyes full of life had become dull with pain
His smile never fully present but enough to keep others at bay
I barely know him now
It has been years since I saw him
Why is it now that I really see him?
I see it in the pictures
Would I see it in him as a person?
Somehow my heart aches to see that
Maybe because I remember how I cried

Miranda Denny
*Chula Vista, CA*

## A Teacher's Regret

The tinkling of glass breaking
Upon my head
Was just a wisp of a dream.
Do I remember his name and How he surprised me
With the words he couldn't read?
Yes, I do.
He was one of the many
I took time to care about.
Goaded by boys he thought were true,
They turned him against all that I was,
And the air flowed of color all around me
Until someone jerked me out of the way,
I heard my own voice screaming in the distance.
I let dreams of shards of glass cut me for so long...
Pushed away: he's now just a memory I rue.

Carla Horne
*Winterville, GA*

## A Moment More

The soul doth sigh for Heaven fair,
God's wondrous face behold;
I long to laud the Lord of Hosts
While walking streets of gold.
To tarry here a moment more,
Then with Him we shall reign;
To be with Christ or live as Christ:
Both magnify His name.
Although this earthly tent constrains
The soul to cursed ground,
On soil the toil is not in vain
In His work I abound.
Be still, O troubled soul of mine,
The kingdom's path a slope;
Though feeble tread ye on this earth,
Thou hast an anchored hope.
To tarry here a moment more,
Then with Him we shall reign;
O Sovereign, 'til Ye beckon me,
On Earth hence I remain.

Amber Lowrance
*Portland, TN*

## Regret

I look at the horizon as I drown in thought. Remembering a pain and suffering that I shall not forget. There was once a time when such pain and suffering didn't exist. A time when I would be stabbed but not bleed. A time when I would suffocate but not drown. A time when a wound only meant another scar. Those were the days before I met you. You had always been there I just never noticed. I would just do what I thought was right. It seemed to be genuine. But you assured the contrary. Of course, sooner than later our paths had to cross. But I wish that time had never come. At first, I was curious who you were. Then I started to get scared. I was afraid of who you really were, so I ignored you as if we had never met. Ignoring you didn't solve anything, I had already met you and what's seen cannot be unseen. That's when it all began. That's when I started to question those closest to me, the rightness in my actions, and the truth behind my own beliefs. And little by little I was ripped away from who I was. I could only feel the pain as I was abandoned by those precious to me. And suffer in the loneliness that you left me.

Brayan Tagle
*El Paso, TX*

## The Cabin in the Woods

I pass the cities and I pass the towns,
Headed North on the North bound.
I exit the four lane, now it is two,
I smell the country, the skies are more blue.
With the city behind me I continue to roam,
The back roads are calling, calling me home.
The stresses reducing, my thinking much clearer,
I continue my journey, dust cloud in my mirror.
I'm headed for two lanes, way off the grid,
Where rivers run wild and secrets are hid.
I exit the vehicle, and take to the trail,
That will lead me to peace, it's my holy grail.
A spiritual place, where nature abounds,
My pine log temple, with no one around.
I enter the cabin, unload my pack,
Move the rocker to the porch, and thank God I'm back.
A light rain is falling, the sun fights to break through,
The clouds open up, a rainbow's in view.
An eagle soars over to welcome me home,
The spirits are with me, I'm never alone.
I long for the wilderness, and I always will,
Mother Nature the artist, the canvas, the paint.

Scott Wolbers
*Perry, MI*

## Getting Over It...

Raped, get over it
Abused, get over it
Advice given by those
Never experiencing the heartfelt woes
Get over it
Words repeated without forethought
Consideration, or empathy
Said by the inexperienced and the many
Not understanding, how just a smell
Can drag a person back to the hell
Again forced to taste that disgusting kiss
Get over it
Words repeated without forethought
Consideration, or empathy
Get over it, reverberates still
Of love taken from thy will
Forced to cower upon the ground
To take every inch or every pound
There is NO getting over it
When memory recall is the culprit
Triggered by smell, action, or sound
A macabre part of life, they're all around
In subtle, to shocking and haunting things
Returning bad memories is what it brings
Reliving the embarrassment, reliving the pain
Of being black and blue, and reliving the shame
So please take note how these words are cut-throat
The pain is real, the drama engraved
The unwilling victim cannot be saved
By those unsympathetic three little words
So please heed these bywords
There is nothing we dream of more
Than to simply move on getting over it

Kristine Petrone
*Nanticoke, PA*

## Time Flies

Time Flies, o'er Earth's highest mountains and lands greatest lakes,
And in the mornings, so gallantly us it awakes.
Making years pass,
Time is Earth's hour glass.
Swooping through each city,
Picking up all of past pity.
Coming in unexpected,
As if it's not self directed.
Time Flies, making seconds come by faster,
Being our futures master,
Picking up all memories as it comes by,
Showing us to new events, is it's way of telling us bye.
To be, or not to be, that is the question,
Will the past events come back to visit the present?
Will the memories stay the same?
To see the clash of forgotten fame.
And the days back then,
Might never repeat again.
Might never show their face,
In other's heads, it took it's place.
CLASH as the remembrance visits us,
Our friends gave them our diligent trust.
The things we remember and value most.
Passed down to the original host.
What we know and what we can imagine,
Laying right beneath our very own chin,
Is now safe with those who shall re-experience it to say,
And live it to our exact, the same start of a day.
Time Flies, I guess, when fun combines with learning,
Time Flies, I guess, against our will and yearning,
Nothing to contradict, Time Flies, comes by every year,
From the start, to the end, the successful cheer.
*Shakespeare's Hamlet

Oliver Bozhko
*Chicago, IL*

## Winsome Spirit

Icicle prisms sunlight bending cause those
frozen crystals brittle to loose their grip from
spire and steeple these cascades shatter, a de-
crescendo we fear their falling, vapor's darlings
they rise again, assume new form.

James Bedinger
*Fairfield, IA*

## War

I see row after row of sleeping soldiers
sleeping underneath crosses I try to keep my composure
as I look around I'm transported somewhere
where there's bodies scattered on the ground
the sound of gunfire and yelling surrounds me
as I look out on the battle scene
the scent of blood is in the air
and I wish I was elsewhere
as I look out on this nightmare
all I can do is think of the Lord's prayer
and as I'm transported back to Arlington
I hear the sound
of twenty-one shot being shot from a gun.

Angela Woodward
*Burley, ID*

## Love Isn't What It Seems

Loving someone who doesn't love you back
Is like bathing in boiling water
Full of pain and hurt, sorrow and regret
Shock and stupidity
Redness takes over like anger and fear
It burns and seems to melt your flesh
You lose your mind over him or her
But what do you get in return
Nothing but rejection and being ignored
And how fair is that
You seem to not exist
You are a ghost in a world of living souls
Your world is a shadowy dark forest
That seems to be a maze
To find the right match to feel existent again

Skylie Gehrls
*Casey, IL*

## Twins

You're my other half
Because one plus one is two,
And I'm single just like you:
So I'm happy that's what's true
Because there's nothing I'd rather be
Than the other half of you.

M-G DiAgostino
*Berwick, PA*

## Recognized Flag

American flag sways
in the sky on the medal pole
this recognized flag
honored by
americans and citizens
as we remember the soldiers
beyond the free United States of America
like a
world-famous soldier
that served our brave country
hereafter

Vincent Bogucki
*St. Joseph, MI*

## Untitled

I bottle up my emotions
like a ship in a bottle
a lost message at shore
but my bottle is made out of thin glass
some people easily break that glass
to see what's inside
and read the message they were never supposed to hear
the ones who need to read my plea
never touch the glass
because of the people who break the bottle
it gets swept away by the current

Meranda Ziegler
*Reading, PA*

## Downward Fall of My Upward Spiral

I want to talk about a boy
When I say boy I mean boys as in plural as in the many boys that have come into my life
I want to talk about how all of them touch me in a way that I cannot explain
I want to talk about how they left a mark on me whether it be good or bad and it did affect me in some way
I want to talk about how bitch became such a repetitive word and how it rolls off the tongue so easy
How it means I'm heartless when you say I'm a bitch
Do you mean it's because I do not trust in the words you speak when you lie to me
I want to talk about how it took me three years and one year of being in an abusive relationship to realize I needed to talk about the man who raped me
How settling for someone who did not love me as much as I loved myself was not okay
How I still sleep with the lights on and door open because I need to know there is an escape
I wanna talk about how I've jumped from lover to lover because I do not feel how I once did
I guess you could say I'm a feminist
When I say feminist I mean sitting in my house alone looking at Facebook of all the girls who posted *me too* but never actually does anything about it
I want to talk about how people tell me to be happy and how other people experience worse things but what they do not understand is that I am a survivor in my own way

Julia Docking
*Cary, NC*

## Cornstalk Soldiers

Golden glow of evening sun
Settles on the cornstalks.
Each one
Stands up tall like a friendly soldier;
Bronze and brittle in the breeze,
Yet noble,
Saluting me as I pass by,
And to every cornstalk soldier man,
I say hi!

Jackie Baker
*Grover Beach, CA*

## Vicarious

Lost in a plethora of elusive dreams
Constantly flashing onto my screens
Living my life oh so vicariously
Seeing another thrive perfectly paradisically
Constantly heartbroken by seeing too much
And my desolate soul always needing too much
Absolutely blinded to what it has done
Joy ripped from our souls until there's none
Brains in harmony of consumption
We are fully lost in an assumption

Emily Wilson
*Tyler, TX*

## Don't Be a Sheep

We live in a world where we march for our lives
Because a little black girl is shot nine times
The name who is blamed is never tamed for their crimes
Never went to jail, didn't even pay a fine
It is a whole twisted system that needs eviction
Death to the people by cops or prescriptions
I'm done with politics and picking sides
We need to come together and save OUR lives
It's not you for you or me for me
It's us against them, you need to see
They divide us up every which way
Left and right politics sound the same
We argue over sports every day and
The brand you rep doesn't have the right saying?
It's crazy, screw the core
Eat off your chain and spit out the norm
Be a free thinker and have your own train of thought
Tired of the government taking without getting caught

Jake Lobdell
*Mesa, AZ*

## Untitled

Sculpt me into something beautiful.
Take me as though
I am a damaged piece of marble,
awaiting your mastered hand
to transform me.

Look at my flaws and feel inspired.
Ready your tools
and turn me into your masterpiece.

Cut me open
then reassemble the pieces,
pliable only to your touch.
Take this raw stone and polish it;
create the rarest gem
the world has ever seen.
I am made of ashes,
but your steady heat
will cause me to metamorphose
into a diamond.

I am here, perfectly imperfect,
but awaiting the effect of you;
the creation of a showpiece,
a transformed being.

Rachel Holt
*Saint Johns, FL*

## When It Ended

You made me carefree like a child,
even in the most stressful times.
You made me feel secure around you,
like it was going to be forever.
You made me love and feel for you,
like I've never done before.
You made me wonder how I would live,
and knock on our father's holy door without you.
When you told me the news, I didn't respond (If I don't say
anything maybe it won't be real). I never understood why.
Why you had to go and make our forever dead and gone.
Why you had to shatter the trust I had in you.
What did you think was going to happen? (I knew I wouldn't
get over you).
Pretend like the past years didn't happen? (I vividly recall those
times and our connection).
I thought I had a place in your life, where you needed me and
I needed you.
(It seems like I'm the only one that needed anything).
It was pointless to try and assure you otherwise,
but you said that what we had gone cold.
And that it just wasn't right anymore.
When I thought that this was worth another try (where we could
have started over).
But I got sick of crying, smiling, and trying for you.
I used to try to get your attention and as close to you as possible,
but now I keep my distance because that was the reality.
I'm exhausted, you drained me of everything, so what could I do?
I just stopped it all, all at once
(I had to convince myself I didn't love you).

Luana Daluz
*Roselle Park, NJ*

## Atlas

I hear everyone I love wail in my ear
I feel all their stress, their sadness, their fear
I hang my head low so they can't see my tears
I start to feel my breaking point drawing near
I can't shut them out, nor can I turn away
I hold the sky on my shoulders day after day
And as everything falls apart, I can only pray
That sooner, not later, they'll all be okay

Zoe Barron
*The Villages, FL*

## Soul Searching

My soul budged at wanting to achieve,
all because I couldn't believe,
in my self and in others,
they didn't understand,
what it felt to take a stand.
I was alone and felt unloved,
until I saw the answer from above.
I couldn't simply walk away,
from what I received that day.
To my surprise, when I opened my eyes,
what I had to face was my demise.
The answer that I seek was here all along,
I had to figure out what was right from what was wrong.

Kristin Ott Peavey
*Canton, MI*

## Smile, in C Minor

Her smile is like an overplayed song
That leaks slowly from her lips
Trickles down the back of her neck
And then wraps around you just like this

The first verse pulls you in close
And promises so much
It's a flash of pearl-white teeth
And a single-handed touch

A thousand voices merge into one
To sing the chorus though a little sharp
Full-bodied, messy, loud, and heavy
But nevertheless warms your heart

Verse two has had too much booze
And sways back and forth on her feet
Climbs on the table to escape her fears
And into your arms, she leaps

And when the highest note approaches,
You see her purse her lips real tight
Trying to hide the cracks in her voice
Because she wants just to forget, tonight

She falters and crashes panic behind her eyes
Then, after the song ends with the crash of drums
You reach out to try and catch her eye
But she disappears with the guitar's last strum

Lily Ding
*Wallingford, CT*

## Life Doesn't Scare Me

Shadows on the wall
Noises down the hall
Life doesn't scare me at all
Bad dogs barking loud
Big ghosts in a cloud
Life doesn't scare me
Mean old mother goose
Lions on the loose
They don't scare me
Dragons breathing flame
On my counterpane
That doesn't scare me at all
I go boo make them shoo
I make fun when they run
Life doesn't frighten me at all
Not at all
Not at all
Life doesn't scare me at all

John Laudman
*Scotch Plains, NJ*

## If Love Was a Lie

If love was a lie,
It would deceive you.
How betrayed you would be!

If love was a lie,
It would fool you.
How senseless you would be!

If love was a lie,
It would be cruel to you.
How unhappy you would be!

If love was a lie,
It would be unfair to you.
How prejudiced you would be!

If love was a lie,
It would trick you.
How ignorant you would be!

If love was a lie...

Kat Cunningham
*Hayden, ID*

## Now I Know

I never knew love could be so happy or sad.
Sharing everything you have good or bad.
I never knew
Love could make you tingle so much.
When that special person you're with
Gives you the slightest touch.
I never knew love was all about respect.
And never hurting each other
Or show neglect.
I never knew love was about give and take.
To always listen to each other
And never be fake.
I never knew love could keep me going
And put a pain in my heart
When you're far away .
I never knew love could be so strong.
Every minute away from you
Is a minute too long .
I never knew love was so intertwine.
Like leaves on a tree or grapes on a vine.
I never knew love could be so true..
Only because
I never knew until I met you.

Lisa Taylor
*Beloit, WI*

## To Love

To Love is to love completely
Unconditionally and without cause
To live is to live fearlessly
No regrets and no applause
To wait is to wait patiently
Unnoticed unrecognizable flaws
To give is to give generously
Without recognition or societies laws
To see is to see the beauty
That creates happiness because
To have is to have unapologetically a hand that never withdraws
From the heart that beats so fiercely
And breaks and mends and bleeds
With a soul fueled by fire and humility
That will always find home just follow where love leads
For a spirit never crushed nor cradled
By the unkind to suit their needs
To forgive without hesitation
Those who seek selfish greeds
To be is to be simplistically
To have reason to succeed
To fulfill your legacy
Without judgments to mislead
Your hearts will to not concede.

Rachel Vaughn
*Willard, MO*

## Bubble

you tried to keep me in a bubble,
always at arms length,
so I was there when you wanted me,
always playing your game.
but the thing you never bothered to learn,
is that I cannot be contained.
I do not need love fed to me
in order to keep me sane.
and the thing about bubbles,
that you must've forgot,
is no matter how much soap you use,
bubbles are meant to pop.

Olivia DeBenedictis
*Naperville, IL*

## Nymph Runes

The devils hindmost
Her eyes compare the illuminating sun
The misty blackness consuming
To conserve her inner mortality
Her wings pure scenery  of a honeysuckle
And mine an inky black hole
Love perseveres in an ember cocoon
It bends to unknown
balance of witchcraft.

Samantha Oglesby
*Ballwin, MO*

## In the Eyes of Hyacinth

Whenever the darkness surrounds you,
little flower,
don't forget how the sun feels against
your beautiful, worn out petals.
Whenever the sun runs you dry,
don't forget how oceans of water
revives your roots once upon a time.
Whenever oceans have drowned and spit
you out like a waste,
uplift yourself, little flower.
Even if you can't support the weight of
your suffering, your pain, your insecurities
learn to forgive yourself...
Learn to forgive yourself of the burdens and all
the wrongdoing.
Because even if you can't,
I'll love you the same.
I'll care for you, I'll tend to you.
I'll be your sun, I'll be your water.
Forever but Never Always,
Past Self

Christelyn Larkin
*Houston, TX*

## For Evil to Flourish, It Only Requires Good Men to Do Nothing

Evil flourishes around us all day
And all it takes is good men not to say
Anything about what they have heard
They just sit there, listen, and ignore it which is absurd
This quote is very important to me
This is because it is part of our future, and was of our history
If I realize what can happen if you don't stand up for
things that aren't right
I might see just the slightest of things and want to fight
Way before the Holocaust when Hitler used a platform to speak
Many people were listening and their interests were peaked
The deeper thinking of Hitler is what the people didn't realize
That Hitler was an evil, evil man starting to despise
All of the people that were not like him, so he started a plan
To kill everyone not like him from child, to woman, to man
All of the people at Hitler's speeches that sat and did nothing
Were witnesses that led to a world, tragic, thing
If the people at those speeches would have just stood up and spoke
Maybe the power of Hitler could have been revoked

Payton Asbury
*Boca Raton, FL*

## The Field

Standing in a field so fair;
Sun gleaming off the dew;
Fog rising up to meet the sky
To start the day anew
My mind begins to wander
To years of long since passed
If any foot has ever stood
Where I'm standing in the past?
Have their eyes ever looked upon
The beauty God has made
And stand in total silence
Like I'm standing here amazed?
There's beauty in the mountains;
There's wonder in the trees;
Like brushstrokes in a painting;
Colors flowing through the breeze
If there was a person
Who was standing in this space,
Did they stop to see the grandeur
And the glory of this place?
I stand here in amazement,
In this land of long ago,
And take in God's creation
In the warmth of morning glow.

Greg Franklin
*Bessemer, AL*

**Friendly Reminder**

Sometimes you need a friendly reminder.
About what you might ask?
You and everyone around hide behind twisted masks.
You try and fit in and wear the latest wear.
You fix your faces to cover up what's really there.
You believe your head even though it speaks lies.
You believe your ears but falsehood it cries.
You do your hair to match the new look for today.
You try it on though it's not going to fit, pay anyway.
You want to be skinnier though you are already slim.
Why you are at it, give your hair a trim.
Tears you cry when you alone because you're afraid.
Your emotions will never be clear like cellophane.
So take of your mask and throw it away.
That friendly reminder might just save the day.
If you still don't believe me, pick back up your mask.
If you have any questions don't bother to ask.
Put it on forever and fit in with the crowd.
Like Dr. Sues says.
"Why blend in when you are born to stand out?"

Melissa Smith
*Hillsville, VA*

## Perfect Combination

A marriage made in heaven then pass down to earth.
Music and poetry is like medicine for the mind, body and soul.
Two soulmates meant to be to together for a lifetime.
Just a few minutes of your time to help you relax
and put you in that right frame of life love mind and mood.
For whatever you need to do, multi task if you need to,
many times Lord knows we have to.
Like love at first sight, you just know deep down in your heart
when something is right.
Especially when God Jehovah send it in Jesus name your way
what the Towntaker Poet calls a everyday blessing .
Thank you i must be doing something right in my life.
The right combination husband and wife , love and happiness
and the list goes on.
But my favorites are lovely ladies ,music and poetry those are my
lovers but God first music and poetry that's my lovers worldwide
a perfect combination.

Curtis Johnson
*Jackson, MS*

## Emotionally Jailed

The white walls and blank mirror
give me a chance to clear my head
As I feel the sickening push of tears
that fill me with dread
My eyes start to water
and I try to hold back
but it's too late;
the water pushes forth and cracks
Fueled by past memories and cruel emotions,
it flows
It crashes into the nearest ship
and takes it below
The water swirls inside my mind
until it overtakes me and I go blind
There's no one there to pull me to the surface
I've closed myself too much for there to be anyone left
I realize this as I accept my fate of a certain death
How did I let myself get this far?
I'm the one who shut myself in and pulled the jail bar
I snap back into reality and look at the bathroom flood
that I'm trying to navigate and get out of
I finally leave it, wishing it a see you soon
Because I know I'll be back before noon

Shanon Kloth
*Winter Haven, FL*

## Halloween

Halloween.
The time of year when the land of the
living
and the land of the dead collide.
Who am I then?
The boy who was born in the collision.

Oliver Stutler
*Deland, FL*

## Untitled

I LOVE SWEETS I love sweets,
I always have.
Chocolate, cake, and candy.
All are just dandy. Any kind, anywhere,
they are all my favorite
food group.
I love sweets. I can't eat them anymore,
as I'm a diabetic. It's so pathetic.
Still, I can dream.
I love sweets! So, eat them while you can.
Don't put it off.
I'll give you a little nudge.
Go ahead! Eat more fudge.

Connie Sarwinski
*Columbus, KS.*

## This

I've never been held until I felt your arms around me. I've never been kissed until your lips were pressed against mine. And I've never felt love until our very first night together. Or maybe I've felt these things before, but they feel different with you. I collapse to your touch, I become an ocean. Your movements make waves in my blood just as the moon does to the sea. And when I start to feel like I'm drowning, your kiss brings life to me.
So when I say I've never kissed before, I mean I've never kissed like this. I've never felt this. I've never craved the touch of another person in the ways that I crave you. And every day you leave me wanting more.
As you sleep I lie close to you, awake, listening to every beat your heart makes. And sometimes I whisper that I love you, hoping you'll hear me in your dreams. You see, I've never loved like this. That scares me. Maybe one day I'll wake up and the waves you once created will lie stagnant. You won't be there to pull me up for air. Or maybe I'll wake up and find myself in a storm of your love. A tempest of devotion and passion.
And I've often wondered if love was enough. But that question doesn't cross my mind anymore. Because this is enough.
I've never been loved until you loved me like this

Angelina Lacroix
*Lake Villa, IL*

*To the man who showed me what love is supposed to feel like, I hope our journey never ends and we continue to love each other for the rest of this life and the next. I love you, Harley.*

## Breaking Point

The horizon is just filled with mist,
But as I look closer there's a twist.
It's covered and covered with black hills,
Making me feel lost in the thrills.
Do not be swayed by such emotions,
For then you'll see yourself devoted.
To something oh yet so dreary,
You cannot find yourself even cheery.
It'll take and it'll take,
While your mind starts to break.
You won't find yourself noticeable,
While others are so lovable.
Into this heap of mess I cause,
When all I can do is pause.
Because then I get my answers,
And suddenly none of it matters.
You'll start to question,
What has caused such depression.
But you'll soon see my dear,
As we'll not be here next year.

Eden Kesner
*Cornelius, NC*

*I'm sixteen years old. I have felt proud of my poems over the years and have decided to publish them. What inspired my poem(s) is my life and feelings. I find no use in poems that don't have a connection of sorts to the author. So I write about what goes on in my mind. Some may call it paranoia or maybe racing thoughts. Those are the things that influenced "Breaking Point." In reality, I took away a whole stanza in order to publish it.*

## Saline Anvils

My shoulders are perpetually wet
with the tears of others
tears I refuse to cry for myself.
Maybe that's what makes me such
a good place to deposit salty sadness.
I have banished my own
and therefore have endless room
for others'.

But the dam is breaking.
These shoulders cannot bear the weight
of these saline anvils
without first caving and heaving
and healing my own.
I must go away for a while
and I am sorry.
I hope I do not regret this.
But I either leave or die
trying to keep you alive.

Anna Gordon
*Nashville, TN*

## Becoming

what I need will come
my vision, my path, my next step
it will come
I believe it will
I send positive hopeful thoughts
prayers
to the One who hears them
and He helps me
leads me and molds me
into a new creation, a masterpiece
perfect and pure
it will come
I know it will
for He gave me the vision
the next step
down the path that leads
to whom I am meant to be

Mackenzie English
*Ravena, NY*

## Firefly

Freshmen in college, friends in M.W. book club
We traveled for the first time to the countryside.
Attracted by starlight and sounds of the stream river.
Walking together outside along the
country road at night.
Caught sight of many glowing fireflies.
Flying between stars in the night sky were
twinkling fireflies.
Saw them for the first time in my life.
One flew carefully so close to my nose, that
I tripped over a stone.
One young man's powerful hand
held my wrist tightly to pull me up.
My heart beat trembled at that moment.
Touched by a young man for the first time,
I was born. My pulse was so loud. I tried to hide it from him.
I ran toward another firefly,
so all he could see was my back.
So many years have passed since those days.
His innocent face with big eyes.
I wonder where he is now, what he is doing now.
I want to walk in the countryside one more time.
Wishing to go back those days.

Myoung Soo Kim
*Fremont, CA*

## How to Be a Hero

If life has chosen its own path for me
I will do just the same
This body is a soldier's
And this fear is not to blame.
This soldier breathes in confidence
He exhales the coward he had been
His home is now the battlefield
And not in Michigan.

Elyse Hopfe
*Pearland, TX*

## Hiding

loose resentment
the kind you forget
until you're reminded
when they make you upset
below-the-surface anger
a dangling threat
dying to explode
all you see is regret
a short grace period
maybe two or three days
but when it returns
you are left in a daze

Lexi McDonald
*Palmyra, PA*

## World

Welcome to the world we live in
Where everything others say gets under our skin.
Some children grow up in this world feeling so alone.
Wandering the streets with no home.
Some children are not even on this Earth by age eleven.
They have already been taken up to heaven.
It is one thing to watch our would crumble,
It is another to stare at others as they stumble.
We need to join together as one
In order to end all wars that have begun.
The world is in desperate need of a change.
The way we are living now is rather strange.
With people dying every day,
There has to be another way.
It is up to us to do what is right,
And I intend to fight with all my might.

Johnna Gallo
*West Warwick, RI*

## You

You are a glitch
Since the day of your birth
You've had zero worth
Yet your still here
How can you even look in the mirror
You are such a disgrace
I can't stand to see your face
You're a fake friend
With fake feelings
You can't do anything right
Your life revolves around bad events
And sad attempts
You used to want to die
Cuts ran down your thigh
Forgot you had friends
You wanted it all to end
I gave up on you
And i wished you did too

Makayla Sloan
*Texarkana, TX*

## Wings

After many attempts and failures to sustain flight,
a young bird leaves the nest once again and attains
flight after just a few minutes, he chirps to tell
mother "LOOK AT ME".
he waves to tell her with his outstretched wings.
At that moment a Monmouth shadow filled the
sky and swoops down and the little bird vanished
without even the littlest cry.

Richard Micallef Jr.
*Kingston, NJ*

## Arrogance

As I sit singing the blues while I'm sitting, shining shoes But as I look as
the rich man proceeds to be mean Thinking, oh nothing can touch me.
But as he rises to pay me so cheaply,
Turning to go strolling down the street,
Thinking very inconsiderably also very unsocially,
He's acting as he's on the top of the line,
Able to do as he desires no matter if it causes fire
As he walks by, the flames just grow higher, stronger and broader As I
watch him leave very stupid and rudely
As he walks, popping his collar,
Thinking he's all that, I just keep quiet
And turn back to my shoe pack.

Edward Reggie Guerrero
*Phoenix, AZ*

## Feeling the Heat

Her touch
Shows no mercy
Just like an Arsonist
It only takes striking one match
The orange glow of gluttony in her eyes
Setting my whole world on fire
The flames dance in delight
Burnt in my mind
Her touch

Jennifer Carr
*Santa Fe, NM*

## For My Heart

The ghastly hand of death has rung my bell;
The final order seeks to serve its vow;
I'm stuck with tolls of nauseous, noxious knells;
The spectral beacon tempts my sombre brow.
My mind conjectures past the edge of life
With anxious thoughts of death's reality
For no elixir halts the eldritch knife;
Whose blade shall slash the roots of every tree,
My world - it fades much like a closing scroll,
But lo! - The raging beating of the heart
Is the incessant knocking of the soul,
And here's my single wish before I part.

Frank Colabella
*Howell, NJ*

## Her

The field gives all the nutrients to crops
While she gives all her breast milk to children.

The field is empty after the harvest
While her children grow up and move out.

The field loses its crops to the farmer
While she loses her breasts to cancer.

The field loses its memory of
richness and harshness of seasons
while her memory is eaten away by Alzheimer's.

The whispering wind comforts the field
with the promise of spring and new life
While children's laughter comforts her
with the promise of grandchildren and happiness.

Nothing can take away a mother's love.

Geum Heui Kim
*Germantown, MD*

## A New Love Unearthed

Flowing thoughts once dispersed,
anticipation met with famished embrace.
Tingling beneath the soul retained grace,
a here today and yearning blaze.
Gleaming feverishly for a peaceful gait,
without the bounds, without detest.
Envisioning the pristine taste,
of energetic but serene gauge.
To concede with courage,
to quiver with chaste.
Entrenched we befitted,
as our journeys fused.
Dawdling with adulation,
and yet with haste.
Enflamed with craving,
from long withered eons,
and malnourished depths,
a new love unearthed,
a union was made.

Maritza Santana
*Orlando, FL*

## Shea Butter

Can I get a brotha
A strong one
A righteous one
A black one
One whose skin glistens
Moisturized and all mine
At night in his durag, no shirt
While I lay on his back..... massage it in
My love
My hopes
And dreams
Of everything I know he is to me
I run it across his arms that hold me
His back that carries me
The golden substance that melts between
My fingers bind us
With you I feel more than lust
Let me rub it through your hair
As I mentally connect us
It shows your inner light
That draws me
Two black diamonds
We shine at night

Akira Strong
*Memphis, TN*

## Winter in My Heart

Your presence is like summer, warming the mountains of my heart
As the snows thaw and flow downstream
Carving a path into the landscape
I too, am altered
And like the rivers steady progression to the ocean
My spirit also presses forward
Only I am transcending to you
Your absence is like fall, sweeping across the valleys of my heart
As the leaves color changes
Transforming the landscape completely
I too, am changed
And like the fallen leaves that the winds have scattered
Like tempered glass shattered
I am broken for you
Your presence is like spring, blossoming over the fields of my heart
As the tall grass sways
Bending with the breeze
I too, am moved
And like the flowers delicate fragrance lingers there
Your scent also fills the air
And I am searching for you
Your absence is like winter, fallen over the forest of my heart
As the great trees stand firm
facing the elements head on
I too, stand strong
And like the branches that reach up to Heaven
In a silent protest to gravity
My hands also make their ascension to the sky
Only I am reaching for you

Tami Rusconi
*Albuquerque, NM*

## Reader

I am not a knight
I am not a soldier
I am not an adventurer
I am not special
I am not important to a plot
I can't go on adventures
I can't go slay dragons
I can't go to castles to save a princess
I can't go traveling with dwarfs and wizards
I wish I could go flying with dragons
I wish I could go swimming with mermaids
I wish I could sing with elves
I wish I could go play with wild and dangerous animals
I cannot do any of these things
For I am not a hero
Nor am I a protagonist to an epic tale
But I am a reader and that is even better

Neiva Hawkins
*Napa, CA*

*I am a thirteen-year-old middle-schooler who is obsessed with reading. One of the reasons I love books and stories so much is because they have gotten me through some of my most troubling times.*

## Dear Mom

Dear mom
The day you died
My heart was torn in two
Can't forget that day even if I tried
I watched your breathing all night
Trying to push my fear aside
I layed in that recliner
Frozen on my backside
Just watching for your breath
Praying it would never subside
Morning came and my nightmare began
Heaven came for you and I cried
And cried and cried.
Now I dream of all things
Left unsaid.
You have your wings
But I felt I couldn't move.
I wish to tell you I understand
Understand the struggle
The strength it took
To raise the wild child I was
The perseverance you showed
The honesty you expressed
The determination you instilled in me.
If I could get one wish
I'd wish for a phone call
To tell you how much
I thank you for it all
I wouldn't be who I am without you.
I've been able to handle the rains downfall.
The sun will come out again
But won't shine as bright without you.

Cheryl Gillis
*Cambridge, MA*

## Allegheny Sky

I am a star gazer, looking up at the vast sky above me
Feeling so big and so small at the same time
Surrounded by love and smiles but seeing none
In the dark of the night
I am the burning embers from our last fire together
Moving silently in the dark
Brushing hands and shoulders, holding back tears
I am the memories hidden in the trees
Where we learned so much about ourselves
Where we first met
Where we said our hellos and our good-byes
I am the stream
Build me up and take me down
We learn our lessons and here they stay
Until midnight comes and we are sent away

Jessica Hockler
*Wappingers Falls, NY*

## Merry Moment

The tree grows greater every year
Holidays are a feat to celebrate
When the atmosphere is sincere
Stories to catch, faces to meet

Let's dance to this soothing beat
The relationships we foster draw us near
Uncover your scars
Now, we can apply the cream of cheer

Parents and grandparents all in one room
Don't make a fuss, it's only until noon
The dog barks like the gifts are here
Little does he know

Some of us have been naughty this year
Still, coming together
Makes me smile
Stay please, even if it's for a little while

Adedamola Adebayo
*Miramar, FL*

## Personal

My laughter takes me over as you fill my
favorite cup
You choose to play my favorite song on the
radio when I think my day can't get worse
Every time I lay my head to sleep, you're ready to
rescue me if anything try's to disrupt my
rest
We stride in perfect harmony as our spirit's
collide into your vast beauty of collected
stupendous roads of gold
What we share feels like the kiss of your first
love or the way you're sick and your mom touches
you and you instantly feel better
Intimacy and romance sweep me as I fall on my
knees over the words you speak
When you call me princess I know
I'm yours
You've had me from the beginning as soon as
you walked into my life I knew there was no way you
could walk out

Mirinda McKinney
*Oklahoma City, OK*

## Mercy Me

The state of the world today is not cool at all
We have the man in charge determined to build a wall
as he appears to keep us safe that's the plan
No drug dealers, killers
but visions like the Klu Klux Klan
Promised to cut funds from the sanctuary city
Appeal Obamacare and cut healthcare for many
Big insurance companies get rich off healthcare
While uninsured struggle and get treatment nowhere
Take out the artificial boundaries
and the artificial lines he say
A few changes made but they remain still until this day
Gov. shut down people can't get no pay
Leaders acting like a toddler can't have it's way
Compromise is what is needed the most
Instead its no humility, or compassion
And the comedians continue to roast
We are laughed at and considered a joke
while Washington play tug-a-war
We struggle and continue to go broke

Shauna Williams
*Raleigh, NC*

## Courageous

The conceptions of feelings and emotions.
Figuresly inclusive to all for which is surrounded by.
Consisting and continuously vibrant .
Universal colors that mind an body can feel an see.
Continuously with no fear, kissing the horizon.
Moving throughout surfaces an counter set's atmospheric.
Courageous evolvement heated like the fire of the sun.
Heated with the passion filled with the courage.
Of the universe never ending an always conspicuously .
Changing into the deep of courage. The courage to
Live , courage to exist.

Bryant Thorpe
*Magnolia, AR*

## Fall

My eyes become painful as my tears fall down my face. As if a waterfall was giving its last drops. I always thought being different was good,but too different becomes painful. Especially when you look different so no one wants to give you love. The love you need to live. So your heart aches. The emotional pain becomes mental and the mental pain becomes physical. So physical that it hurts to the point of wanting to scream. But instead you look for someone and when you don't see anyone it reminds you you're alone. And it all starts over again and won't stop until you find someone or become broken

Alyson Camplain
*Corpus Christi, TX*

## Gun of a Son

Maxson,
What are you packing?
Is it a gun?
Boy don't be so dumb.
Put that thing down.
Guns are for clowns.
Come spend some time with me
I can show you peace & tranquility.
You're almost twenty.
Let me show you how life is suppose to be.
What you see, when you're at the movies
Is how I feel you been acting.
Son, please momma don't want you packing.
Hang with family, they'll guide you right.
Just don't be a pistol packing,
Graveyard stacking,
Son of a gun.
When you're suppose to be out having fun.

Maria Clavo
*New Orleans, LA*

## Castle in the Sky

A castle in the sky,
So way up high,
For people to see,
Time and time again.
A castle of whites,
With peace and no frights,
And bays of blues,
With no else to pick or choose.
This one white castle,
No move forcing a hassle,
Floating up there,
Broadcasting no resistant air.
The big and the fluffy,
The huffy and the puffy,
A white ball fit for royalty,
Of utmost the highest quality.
My finger falls down,
On my face the opposite of a frown,
Staring at a cloud,
That screamed big and loud.
The castle soon disappeared,
And a new castle interfered.
This new castle a dragon,
Sitting inside a colossal wagon.

Lexie Haney
*Mechanicsville, MD*

## What Is in a Rose

Why is it always the grass, the wind, the sun,
That gets written in these eloquent messages for generations.
Why not pierce straight through to the destructive qualities of that which you seek to rebuke?
Address the greed instead of the ivory.
The monarchy in place of the fairy wren.
They have done naught but present themselves as vulnerable to the manipulative pen, that when their name is crowded in with fancy dialect,
taints their celebrity with blood, and murder and death; Mistakes only ascribed to the writer and his company.
Perhaps it is a balm to the stinging slap,
To think that something inanimate is able to be equated with such evil comforts those who have made mistakes,
And becomes the excuse of those who meant it.
But then do the sun, the wind, the grass,
serve their purpose?
There is no way to know.
So we continue to talk about the art of the pen instead of the gun,
which is indeed mightier than the sword.
The pen's standing has yet to be seen.
But until the day when people are addressed by name and the page points to perpetrators,
And there is another sky, that is just the sky,
We can only hope that the grass, the wind, the sun,
helps the heart and not just the mind.

Bracha Gluck
*Brooklyn, NY*

## Bloom

My heart blooms for you
Like a red rose in the warm sun
Petals growing fuller
Soaking up the purest light of life
Where are you in the meantime
This eager in between time
My whole heart waits for you
I can't wait to touch your nose
And kiss your little toes
But first of all and most of all
I cannot wait to find you
The moment that my heart
Will flutter, jump and drop
Fully nearly stop; In awe of you
The moment that I find you
Will be the greatest gift of life
You're all I've ever wanted
My heart blooms for you
Like a red rose in the warm sun
My life will bloom in ways never known
Like a red rose in the warm sun
I cannot wait to bloom with you
As I carry you beneath my heart
In this eager in between time
My whole heart waits for you

Jakiya Clark
*Nashville, TN*

## Metaphorical Depression

Staring out at the horizon line
across a stretch of miles that seem to remain for eons,
looking for something to see,
but nothing to look at.
Eyes full of tendencies to search for one thing
she's able to hold onto, but she just isn't.
The longing feeling of absolutely needing
to have found something,
settling in the depths
of the cold body, that's supposed to be hers.
A wooden box trapping the blood flow,
that used to seep out of the cracks,
but now just fills the box,
with the pressure
until eventually she is going to break.
Another box. Restart. The pale yellow desk,
putting the same force onto the stack of notebooks staring incomplete,
as the blank paper puts back onto the surface.
Words aren't words anymore,
as they've started depending on her
being able to spell them correctly.
Letters stopped being letters
at the same time
that pressure stopped being a physical act.
The beginning of what felt like
the next amazing thing
turning out to be what holds her
down under the ground.

Kaylee Baker
*Mount Vernon, WA*

## Dream Away Yehoshua, Dream Away...

Dreams are the best place I can be...
when I dream, I escape my cruel reality,
the awful reality, the reality where I am tortured, and forced to work...
in my world where I am alone no mama no papa no Moshe or Edit - I am surrounded by four walls - with no escape...
When I dream, I dream of a reality where family and friends do not disappear,
a reality where I am still living in Berlin, where I can go to school, where there is comfort...
but alas, that will not be my reality-no matter how much I yearn for it to be...
my reality will never be the same again; when I wake I will not be surrounded by friends and family -
but by bitter cold and my solitary or perhaps, I won't wake...
Perhaps my dreams are where I am meant to be, where I am safe and where I am free, where can express myself and be who I truly am - where I am treated decently.
At night I cry myself to sleep - wondering why,
what did I do?
There is no one who was German or French...
just Jews, is that really enough to be treated the way I am?
Am I at fault for being Jewish?
At night I hear mother calling my name, "Yehoshua",
"Yehoshua" in her candy like voice... I call out for her but to no avail - she will not appear not today, not tomorrow, not next week, or next month... that is my realization.
Mother always said the promised land is Heaven - but, I realize that she is wrong - the promised land is not Heaven - but dream! the one place where I can escape reality...

Mariel Roa
*Yonkers, NY*

## A Sickly Wood

As far as woodlands go, this is a sick wood,
Saturated with morbid death and bitter decay,
With no more abundance of life and youth than
A graveyard; all is slowly dying and growing gray.
There is no clear footpath for me to follow on,
For the way is strewn with brown, infolded, crisp,
Leaves, which long since lost their strength to
Live upon the now barren trees.
They are dearly missed.
The air is noxious with decay, and the very trees are
Rotting from their innermost rings and deepest
Roots outward.
The whole wood is weak: I know it will fall
If ever should come a storm, gale, or tempest.
Yes, it is an ill wood which I walk in so often.
It is dying, I can see it in the trees.
This forest is beyond saving; it is lost—
It is dying, I can see it in the trees.

Reuben Williams
*Berlin, MD*

## My Mother

Thank God for my mother, her love and her care
Who prays for me daily, all through the year.
When I'm discouraged, burdened or sad,
Mother is always there to make my heart glad.
She reminds me that my Saviour never forgets his own,
She admonishes and encourages me to hold on. Thank God for my mother, who trained me as a child
To love and serve Jesus, who is gentle, meek and mild.
She took me to Church and Sunday school too,
And knelt with me at the altar because she knew
I needed Jesus to make it in this world
Of sin, sickness, cruelty, wickedness and crime. Oh, how I thank God for a mother like mine
Because of her training I've found a Savior divine
I love and respect her, and I know that one day
"Well done, my faithful servant,"
She'll hear the Lord say
"Your task is accomplished, your work is all done
Enter my kingdom and receive your crown. "

Jacinth Wallace
*Newark, NJ*

## Letting Go for Good

When you finally stop hoping
When you realize they're gone
When you finally move on
That's when you remember
Remember the friendship
Remember the words said
Don't forget
Hold on tight
For just a moment
Remember the smiles
Remember the laughter
Remember the happiness
The pain isn't there
Time to let go
To move on
Time to forget
Push the memories aside
You hurt for a moment
Let the tears fall
They are gone
When you finally let go
You forget forever

McKayla Stoddard
*Saint Anthony, ID*

## She Is

Sapphire silk entangles her gorgeous shape
She slumbers with a graceful snore
Her bed is her home
The fine works of nature's hand
Which traced her body with the paints of emerald
And the pencils of a tree swallow's feathers
She is The Ocean  Her fingertips tickle the islands
Her palms hold volcanoes of the deep
Her beauty is entrancing
Her lullaby
Sung by maidens of the sea
A melody of love and death
She is The Ocean  Salt sifts through her hair
A glittering crown
Reflecting the rainbow above
Dissolves into a vast sea
Lost forever in a cup her own poison
A poison apple of her very own
She is The Ocean

Elaria Boutros
*Ellicott City, MD*

## Reflections

As I walk by a window, I glance over
and see a person so lost and lonely
Sitting by the water, I glance over
And see a face so long and blue
I glance down into the sink and my mind takes me away
as I gaze at warm water hitting against my hands
I'm taken to a place within my heart, it's a feeling of
Loneliness, emptiness, and sadness
I look up and see the reflection of me
Wrinkled skin on my face that was once firm and glowing
Gray hair that was once golden brown
I wonder if there is anything I can do
to become youthful like I once knew
What is it I wonder that will heal this broken heart
Is it time that heals
Is it looking younger, feeling healthier
Is it Finding new romance
Who is to know what heals the heart
Perhaps it's not the heart at all
But the mind that must be defined

Linda Deauseault
*Chicopee, MA*

## Pan

Above the windows
beyond the lights
A boy is climbing
the burning heights
He has no map
he's fled his home
He'll surf the wind
and waves of foam
Chasing embers
of ashen clouds
Riding red currents
to meet the ground
and I wait at the window
For his brushing barefeet
to walk upside my house
and I'll peek
and see him surfing
the starry seas

Anthony Miller
*Jamestown, NY*

## I'm Sorry

a little misshapen,
my ball of clay is.
it's small. it's lumpy.
it's easy to miss.
spun round in circles
from morn until noon
it's easily dizzy,
and twirls out of tune.
a nick. a scar.
a faded square there.
left lonely one night,
it couldn't quite fare.
like earthquake, crumbled
in a stranger's hand.
masterpieces, clearly,
never go as planned.
thrown in the fire,
my clay lost its shine.
but i won't apologize,
this clay is still mine.

Olyvia Saathoff
*Rigby, ID*

## Solitude

I'm dying on my own, I'm afraid and alone
One day, I'll leave and nothing will be on my headstone
Solitude's chains hold me back
The void I live in is pitch black
The strain against me causes an everlasting panic attack
Someone comes to help but it just makes things worse
No one can break me from this curse
All they do is preach their heroic verse
I lay here tired and weary
My vision is dark and dreary
People are always distrustful and leery
Can't they see I just need the key
To release me and set me free
I'm fading on my own
I'm afraid and alone
And one day, I'll leave with nothing on my tombstone

Karilyn Blanchard
*Fairbanks, AK*

## Venus Dream

I had touched you in dreams,
Embraced you in thought,
Caressed your lips with mine
Your hair between fingers
Your body with soul.
We fused in my rest
Among the blurry streets of dreams
Beneath a canvass of black.
Our eyes the only voice,
I found you in my mind
In the imagination of nothing
Pulling you from oceans like Venus
And I, Prometheus of our moment.
But it be only that,
A beginning at an end
Fading as we loved,
You dissolving to my waking eyes.
And so I weep
For I know
There shall be no other dream
No other moment among blurry streets,
For you and I.

Micah Biffle
*Marysville, WA*

## This Love

This love I know it so well
Anger, aggression, a hint of depression
My body turns colors and starts to swell
But that's okay, he didn't mean this
After all, he apologized and gave me a kiss
I start to feel comfort
I start to feel in place
But then, who was that you gave your embrace?
"No one.", you say
"You've had a long day.."
"You're not thinking clear."
"What you see is not as it appears."
I shake and think as I try to breathe
But just like that, you make me believe
Am I going crazy?
What I think starts to get hazy
I can no longer trust myself
What I see must be something else
This pain in my chest for being betrayed
It's not your fault, you just held the blade
You promise to change, to be someone better
But that only lasts 1.. 2.. 3.. love letters
I get impatient as we start to grow tense
I can feel it again and it starts to make sense
This cycle started when we first began
This love, I know, was all part of the plan

Aubrey Johnson
*Enterprise, UT*

## The House on the Hill

On a desolate hill,
there is a house with no windows
the floor is blanketed in broken glass.
the remanence of last twilight's indiscretions
leaves its syrupy, poignant smell in the air.
Far off the trees of the surrounding forest signals its own destruction
Closer now, closer, until it has almost reached the house.
But the hill was too tall, too forsaken, too alone, for the sparks to catch.
Better to have been engulfed in orange fingers, than stay
Broken, Worthless, Dirty, Damaged
Better to have been gutted and rebuilt, than to stay
Unfulfilled, Unloved, Abandoned and Defeated
Atop of that God-Forsaken hill.
Decay and Death now infest the house like a plague—
carcasses with wings sleep now in the empty sills
not even the green tendrils of life untouched survive.
gone are the last traces of light
gone are those still, small echos of laughter… another age perhaps.
An age of faithfulness and hope.
An age of promise to be fulfilled.
An age of prosperity.
The tired bones of the aging house creak as if to cry out to the wind
"Eli, Eli, lema sabachthani?"
My God, my God, why have you forsaken me?
The wind says nothing
He dances through the trees the dead grass
And the dying foliage
yet there are no words on His tongue.

Ella Downing
*Highlands Ranch, CO*

## The Desert

My body is a strange desert, empty and vast
it has been explored but not by me
I know not of the blinding beauty and darkness of its dunes
simply what I can put together by the inkling of what I know

Marcela Tordin
*Doral, FL*

## Liquid

Liquid streaming down the glass
Like a crystal clear diamond
Or a highly-polished brass
Gives a glimpse inside
Like a window into my heart
By whether the water's dirty
Or pure from a fresh start
Clear clean water
Only one can give
But the choice is yours
If you want to truly live
If the world looks in what will they see
Muddy dirty waters or God's love for you and me

Grace Barnett
*Canonsburg, PA*

## Vacation

I sit idly by as the masses
flood the splintered planks,
Drop after drop, the sugary ice cream
nestles its way between the wrinkled planks,
into a situation it can never escape.
The boards gasp for air as they're suffocated
by the ignorant cowards hobbling from shack
to shack feeding their addictions.
They all appear irritated, in a place of such joy.
Parents, who could use parenting of their own,
yank their kids towards the boiling sand,
lining them up like prisoners
They shout, "Stand still or no ice cream for you!"
Why?
So all of Facebook can gawk at the fake smiles of
rude children dressed in unison like soldiers,
only playing a part for a promised sugar high, that will never come.

Michael Fiore
*Schenectady, NY*

## Nighttime Walks

"go say hi"
"be polite"
"always exercise so you can maybe have a valentine"
and "remember to never ever go outside during the nighttime".
the things we need to remember as women.
and if we decided to put that advice aside,
we don't suffice as women and we wouldn't be caught, alive the next day.
but women are done having to put on the
disguise of being nice or having to be silent so u can shine
or so others don't feel uncomfortable.
it's time for others to realize being a woman is hard
and sometimes even requires sacrifice.
so if this makes you feel threatened or uncomfortable,
you need to start learning about the women who have put their own
sweat and blood to protest against this,
and see why it is so important that one day we can walk outside, in the nighttime,
without having to run back inside, or
being scared of what hides in the night.
but all in good time.
right?

Evette Palacios
*Big Bear Lake, CA*

*If we don't have equality, then what are we?*

## Lost Socks

I wear my dead father's socks.
They do not guide my steps
like quiet and steady words,
but they comfort my feet
when I slumber, and when I walk.
They are not new socks,
which struggle to stretch around
my thickening calves and ankles,
and leave deep impressions
that fade away while I sleep at night.
And they are not the weathered or worn,
their holes growing larger
with every mile walked, until at last,
my toes burst out and brush
the edges of these cold, leather shoes.
They are my socks now,
filling the empty space
in an unkempt and chaotic drawer.
Pairs and orphans, alike,
fumbling for a place in the here and now,
as if they know, one day,
they, too, will be lost between
the desert and the ocean,
or disappear into the deep recesses
of a dark and dusty laundry room.

Todd Williams
*Rapid City, SD*

## The Sinner's Consequence

A woman is missing all that's left is a piece of her dental.
As I walk to the site, I hand in my credentials.
A young man was found dead,
Her father wants her found, as sorrow fills his head.
I held a letter with beautiful calligraphy.
It tells of his sorrow and the reason for sending me.
I accept the case with feelings of apathy.
The scene of the crime is like a peerless symphony.
Barely any trace of the murderer's biology.
Searching for the slightest mistake or oddity.
On the man's body shows a damning fatuity
Nothing can escape my hyperacuity.
A syringe used by the demophobe,
That will put the dealer under my probe.
There is one man who owns the monarchy
And will sell to anyone who will pay his fee.
I met with him to interrogate and impel
And a house was uncovered at the climax of his tale.
I was soon searching this monotonous house
To find the girl in her ripped and torn blouse.
She cried as her gaze reached me, her face filled with sorrow
For she knew I covered all tracks to follow.
My glee in knowing that her father is in pain was audible
The fact in him thinking I will find his daughter is Ironical.

Stephen Goodwin I
*Memphis, TN*

## Pater Noster

In the afterlife there are no graves,
Or fields of the fallen dead.
No catacombs of weary bones
Where fearsome ghouls are fed.
No monuments to demonstrate
Where the remains that lie beneath,
Gather to them the tears I cry,
As I share with them my grief.
No one wears the wooden coat
In a realm of eternal night,
Instead their mortal coil is shed
As they pass into the light.
There received by the heavenly host,
Are they overwhelmed by grace.
And the ones they lost along the way,
Are once again to them replaced.
Oh My God, Hallowed be thy name which I adore,
Your blessings be upon us all, now and forevermore.
For it's your promise of eternal life,
That lets me know I'm free.
Told to me by the words of Christ,
who came and died for me.

John Thurman
*Pleasanton, TX*

## Imagine a World

Imagine a world with peace
Where there is no violence
And all fighting will cease
Where all mean words go to silence
Imagine a world where everyone is glad
Where everyone will try
A place where no one is sad
A place where no one will cry
Imagine a world where people care
A place where people can be okay
Where everything is fair
Somewhere people can have a good day
Imagine a world with no fear
We all have a heart
And though it may seem unclear
We all have a part

Kearstin Safford
*Gainesville, VA*

## Phoenix

Phoenix phoenix burning blaze
Deadly phoenix fires raze
No immortal burning flame
Could use to fearful forest maim
With what wings dare phoenix fly
Soaring celestial so high
In the fire pit was thee
Thy pain burned strong eternally
The ash was raining down so thick
The fire spread so very quick
And burned and burned and burned and burned
Until the mighty phoenix learned
If he wanted to soar so much faster and higher
He must control his ruthless fire
And when the spark fell and burned bright
It lit the dark and jet black night
But got snuffed out by phoenix power
Which could light night in darkest hour

Chase Testa
*Clinton, NJ*

*I love poetry, rock climbing, and eating good food. Ever since I was little, I have just loved words. I remember one time when my family took a drive, I said "This is a beautiful countryside." I was two. I am an only child and have had to entertain myself a lot so I made up stories and poems about the world around me. Silly, dark, deep, or sad, they all have one thing in common. They are mine.*

## Passion

Love is passion,
Passion is love.
Like wind over oceans,
Blue sky's above.
Your heart is a locket,
A key must be made.
To unleashing emotions,
That will never fade.

Regina Sims
*Spring Valley, CA*

## Showering with Depression

Standing numbly in the shower
The water feels like bullets falling from the sky
As I sluggishly reach for the soap I'm reminded what an anchor is
The small amount of water that pools around my feet feels
like pebbles
This shower is the second most comfortable thing in my life
I'm comforted in the pain it rains down on my because at least
I get to feel something
This nothing that I feel can only be washed away by bullets
My feet firmly planted in the pebbles as I
hold the anchor and let the shower reek havoc on my body

Lilly Owsley
*Pierceton, IN*

## Self-Love

My hair is curly and my thighs are thick
I'm so mean I make medicine sick,
My skin is brown sugar and my eyes are seductive
yet my thoughts are so damn destructive,
I'm a queen and I'm nothing all in a day
I'm here and I'm gone, my mind can't come to play;
I give love so freely, like a bee goes to honey -
pollinating others while my own soul is starving.
I love to feel the sun on my face
but some days I feel I should just go away,
My mind pulls me deeper under the water,
I float in my thoughts, bubbles and a self-loathing daughter,
I push to the surface for a burst of air,
but all I take in is loads of my straightened hair.

Angelina McCahon
*San Diego, CA*

*I currently reside in San Diego, CA and work as a labor and delivery nurse at a local hospital. While I love helping to deliver life into the world, in my spare time I write. Writing breathes life into my soul and I pull from my own life experiences for inspiration. My writing incorporates the realization that came at twenty years of age that I was half black in addition to Italian. I draw from my memories of meeting my biological father and other things that spark my soul like the depths of the ocean or honey's golden hue.*

## An Ode to Our Wahoo

Patiently waiting...
Yay, Wahoos!
Surrounded by crowds of anxious families
Drizzle, dark skies, wet seats, and mud
The walk begins,
Yay Wahoos!
Graduates surging forwarding in a sea of colorful balloons.
The future lies ahead of as
Memories of their past four years reflect in a rear view mirror.
The crowd cheers with excitement.
Yay, Wahoos!
All heads turn to hope to catch a glimpse of their graduate.
I see my sister!
Kelsi, Kelsi, Kelsi!
Our voices ricochet across the hallowed ground
Silence as the ceremony begins
Balloons float heavenward
Pride in my sister and all her accomplishments
My heart is full!
Kelsi, Kelsi, Kelsi, yay our Wahoo!

Kenzie Gardner
*Alexandria, VA*

*That's me, Kenzie Gardner—Cambodian, adopted, athlete, compassionate, welcoming, genuine. Quirky brain = auditory processing disorder. My brain can't hear; it freezes and processing information and facts quickly just doesn't happen. But I have risen above my learning disorder and succeeded throughout my high school career. Shutterbug = photography. #EMU2023/major—photograph! I enjoy perfecting my craft, learning more about art, art history, and seeing the world through different eyes. Urban polo = lacrosse/field hockey (#7). Playing lacrosse for the first time ever for EMU Royals LAX team is an athlete's dream come true. Play hard. Make history.*

## Your Home, Not Ours

You make me feel out of place
Even when I'm doing nothing,
standing next to you I am less
I get judged for listening to your type of music,
Dressing like you,
I get told that I should just be me,
Authentic,
Unique,
But that is nearly impossible to do in a world that you own.
We are different,
In almost every aspect.
You live life to the fullest
I do the same while trying to avoid bullets
That you present us with every now and then
We dance in your shadows
We persevere and try our best to win the fight
But you constantly remind us that we don't have a chance
at least not for a while.

Lawra Gourgue
*Brooklyn, NY*

*I am an African-American high school senior from Brooklyn, NY. In the fall of 2019 I will be attending Pace University, majoring in film. In my free time, I enjoy doing photography and exploring new places. My poem was inspired by the movie "Us" and a lot of issues we see presently in the media.*

## Grey Static

My world is like a movie.
But older, in black and white...
The plot line is weird and rambling. So am i.
They gave me flowers as a gift,
A funny get well soon
The flowers will die,
How ironic, right?
They'll wilt.
All the colors drain out...like Draino
In the mirror, it isn't me,
But I move, and so does she.
It's only a figure, not a girl at all.
Only the eyes are mine, filtered green
It's so pretty, glazed over
Like a donut or cake, or something pink and sweet.
They gave me flowers as a gift, I threw them all away.
Picking them off in a 'he loves me' type cliche.
They wilt in the bin, underneath harsh artificial sun.
And I'll let the colors drain out.
They'll turn and mesh and fold
Into
Grey static
Their dead petals all strobing, in an epileptic fit.
All I see is static
Grey and bleak.

Jordie Cornfield
*Essex, MA*

*I wrote this poem about dealing with depersonalization. When I look in the mirror when this happens, in the mirror it isn't me. The title for my poem "Grey Static" comes from a recurring dream I've had since I was six or seven. I see flashing static against a cartoon house. It's scary, and I do feel that same sense of depersonalization. On a lighter note, I'm fifteen, and I love to read and write and create little worlds. I'm an only child, which you would know by meeting me because I'm super outgoing and love to meet new people.*

## What I've Always Dreamed Of

Little fingers, little toes
Sweet pure eyes and tiny nose.
Strong willed spirit, full of love
These are the things I've always dreamed of
Tupperware thrown all around
Purses filled with anything found
Dressing the dog with dress up stuff
These are the things I've always dreamed of
Toys in every part of the house
Weekend trips to see that mouse
Nighttime prayers to the Lord above
These are the things I've always dreamed of
Teaching how to read and write
Explaining sins avoidable plight
Seeing first hand sisterly love
These are the things I've always dreamed of
Late night talks about this and that
Rearranging the house in two minutes flat
Watching you drive was a little rough
But these are the things I've always dreamed of
Watching you learn through all these years
Lots of laughter and many tears
You are my joy whom I love
You are what I've always dreamed of

Misty Milliman
*Vero Beach, FL*

## Blankets of Bliss

Making meaning of each morning,
Blanketed by bliss,
Captivated by a single kiss,
Surrendered by sultry salutations,
Of her heated passions,
Overcome by a glare,
Seduced by a stare,
And so eloquently expressed,
In each setting with care,
Surely a splendid sight to share.

Justin Trautman
*Fayetteville, AR*

## A Love Letter to the Ghosts

Today a ghost entered me
It did not knock on the door
Or stop to say hello
It went right through almost as if it was never there
No one noticed
I didn't speak
So when it left
They didn't see
All of the pieces it broke
When I said I wanted it to leave
And so it left the pieces for me to clean

Anna Connett
*Woodville, WI*

## Why?

I was just a game to you
And you showed me how it was played
You said you loved me
But those were just lies
I cared for you a lot
But that was my mistake
I walked to our special spot
Trying to say goodbye
I can't keep pretending that you didn't hurt me
Cause you did
I feel so used
And my world is crashing around me
I trusted you
And I just want to know why?
Why me?
Why was I such an easy target?
You said all kinds of things
Just to get what you want
And once you got it
You were out the door
I have zero respect for you
You disgust me
I can't stand to be around you
I hate you and always will

Chelsea Smith
*Bay St Louis, MS*

## Piano

Melodious tunes dance and play around while
Mother glides her fingers magically on the black and white ivory keys
Playing each note with elegance, yet playfulness
If only I'd known
That those same notes that I thought I would recollect with the same joyful memories
Are now poisoned with disappointment
All the once beautiful notes fade away and are now filled with harsh dissonance
If only I'd known
That one day those cherished memories, would be the catalyst of loneliness
That one day those notes and sounds would no longer riff and run with beauty
That one day I would have to live with the muffled sounds of a piano
Now that I know
That life is like a piano with highs like crescendos
Into lows like diminuendos
Yet live on is what we must do

Vinay Hinduja
*Flushing, NY*

## Holding with Silence

When did I start to blur the lines of your skin with the salty ocean wind, covering over my sorrows with all the words possible to wash away the silence that you left me to hold?
I tried to collect every bit of dust that had slipped from your bed sheets that last day, but it wasn't enough to keep your form, your scent alive and lingering upon me whenever I lie down within the dark night.
It is when I sit alone: no book, no friend, no worldly distraction,
that your eyes—that dark brown—your eyes begin to etch their way upon the pavement so that I never forget how your dreams infused their way into the very mold of my brain.

Your shadowed sadness still flows slowly through my veins, your mischievous laugh echoing within the walls that enclose the flesh of my tongue, the hollows that house the glimmering light you brushed into the things you made with your hands.
How often it is that I hear a melancholy song: piano and cello crying together slowly in harmony.
And it is only you for whom I can store away the musical notes, those repetitions that I know only you could decipher and so deeply understand.
How can it be? Explain to me. Tell me how it's possible that what we had wasn't strong enough to cut through the smoke that always hovered so close to you when you slept—your eyes so wide open, unable to break away from the chains you so carefully one day made.

I know that they all say that one can never step into the same river twice.
That life goes on, the past remaining always past and gone.
And yet I catch myself reaching out with my fingertips, trying to feel my way towards that imaginary thread that I envision might just guide me back towards a time when your voice whispered to me with a sound
—a sound that could only have been you—the sound of late autumn leaves.

Eva Garcia-Mayers
*San Diego, CA*
*I have been actively engaged in creative writing and artistic expression for most of my life. Poetry and art have helped me cope with suffering and sorrow, transform pain and loss into something meaningful and better understand myself and the basic human need for love and belonging. Many of the themes in my work revolve around nature, the interconnectedness of the universe; the human condition as mortals living in a changing world; and our search for meaning and spiritual fulfillment. I believe in the transformative power of language; it can create new worlds that can be conveyed and shared with others.*

## Into the Night

I live for the night. I always stay up.
I stay up as others lay down;
I find peace in a sleeping town.
The night time is the right time
to face the dark side of the day.
I like staying up deep into the night.
I feel alive when I walk empty streets.
I love sitting in a row of empty seats.
When I stay up, I see lights turn off.
I am awake to hear something
quickly turn into nothing. I am awake
to bring the only light into the night.
I am here to do my work out of sight.
I live for the night: what can I say?
My light does not shine during the day.

Jesse McDaniel
*Ellensburg, WA*

## Scent of Rain

the scent of "earthy - green"
before coming thunderstorm
twilight rain
serene
glowing rainbow
fading sun
scent of rain on warm asphalt

Dimitra Hutchison
*Colorado Springs, CO*

*"Scent of Rain" was inspired by a special childhood memory and my faith and relation to God. I was born and raised in Germany, but my ancestors are Greek (Minoan). I am proud to be a US citizen.*

## Collision Course

Consuming collide
Cracking, creates chaos
Confronted, and caught

Avery Berg
*Seattle, WA*

*In a mere thirteen years, I've experienced the most torrential trauma I ever will have to in my life. At the age of ten, I was diagnosed with stage four, extremely aggressive, rare brain cancer. A tumor, atypical teratoid rhabdoid tumor, was growing in the center of my head. Hell was consuming my delicate brain. Poetry became an outlet to put all that hell on paper and form beauty of it. Helping my sister write haikus three years later, cancer-free, I thought to write one of my own of truth, love, and pain and solace and rebirth hidden deep between the lines.*

## Common Sense

The sun races westward,
And joins the horizon in ethereal embrace.
Out of convenience,
We remain adjunct.
How greatly is the search mounted
To find the truth,
That which is lost upon the addled corpse
When we perceive the smell?
May our demons dream of only things more worse.
Our brave people are not to be abashed
By the fools who appear in public lacking
Common sense.
The people are more agminate than ever before,
Then adamant in their journey forward.
Beware!
Among us stand those who live,
Only to satisfy temptation and foolish pride.
Their voices will be heard, but are doomed...
To be lost upon the tumultuous winds,
While the birds may explore the sky freely.
Choirs will sing for the dead,
And then more so,
For the glory of God.

Nicholas Gutierrez
*El Paso, TX*

## Speechless

I try to explain to you everything I think about
The good things
The bad things
The happy things
The sad things
I struggle to speak though
To find words that express how I actually feel
To find words that can remove the mask I hide behind
To find words to pull me from the darkness consuming me
To find words that make me feel human again
It is not that I do not want to speak, but that I cannot
Like a bear hides from the cold, I hide from the world
I hide from insecurities, from hatred, from the truth
Only to leave myself amongst a pool of uncertainty
Because overall, I am completely speechless

Shannon Callihan
*Monongahela, PA*

## Nipsey Hussle

Young king taken by a gun
How could that coward take you away from your daughter and son
You took your last victory lap
Nah, that wasn't your last scratch that
Your words will go on in our hearts
You hussled and motivated through your arts
Last time that I checked you were making that change
Dedication to your craft on and off the stage
Grinding all your life to help the streets
Never thought we'll see you under the white sheets
Millions while you young
You always spoke in spiritual tongue
We all saw your vision, it's all loaded bases
Tell us when to run home, don't forget to tie up your blue laces
You built a real big shop in your community
Got Keyz 2 the City, you just wanted unity
Double up on our awareness
Hope your eye sees the unfairness
You're always gonna be right hand to God
Your body might be gone but your soul will never be robbed
We're hungry, revolution on our menus
In your name Nipsey the marathon continues ...

Destinee Merino
*Teaneck, NJ*

## Poison

but my mind bakes potions
just to pool the poison
in cocktail hell hole
well of my head

Erin Burke
*New York, NY*

## The Tide Never Wanes

Crashing and dispersing;
Everlasting motion ceases to exist—
Yet another wave appears in the
Distance as if nothing occurred.
Ready! For the waking impact that one brings
Splashing away, the hopeless desires—
Bouncing away in unorderly joy;
Chaotic rhythms of endless life spew
Into action! Another—
Wave crashes to the shore.
With every crash, every foam—
Every constant disturbance creates
An endless sea of possibilities
Yet the Tide never wanes.

Jonathan Sterrett
*Charlotte, NC*

## Life

It's a fantastic life
A beautiful place
The perfect wife
A perfect place
Then the demon creeps in
Deep in my head
A perfect life
No
Wish I was dead
Not sure what went wrong
My mind is unclear
Once I look down
I see the devil in the mirror
Its not my face
A stranger I've never known
The demon stares back
My addiction has grown
Won't be long now
My brain is ruined
Wife has left
A future uncertain

Joshua Gass
*Fairview Heights, IL*

## Lucky

All of us are lucky.
We are lucky for food.
Lots of people starve
That's what puts me in a bad mood
We are lucky we are healthy
Some people fight for there health everyday
And hoping they can stay.
But sometimes they go off to heaven
We are lucky to have shelter
Over 150 million people don't have a roof over there head and that makes me sad.
Then I look at huge houses I pass bye which makes me mad.
We are lucky we can walk
We are lucky we can talk
We are lucky we can see
We are lucky we can laugh
We are lucky we can play
Don't Take your life for granted,
it might pay off someday.

Louie Castellarin
*Hudson, OH*

## What If

What if I told you that I could not be touched
Not physically but emotionally
What if I told you that I had a barrier around my heart
That I had lost the capability to trust and love
Would you still want me
What if I told you what I really thought about
About how dead I feel inside
About how far I want to run and hide
From the pain that eats at my soul and slowly kills me
I am a person who lives with a pain that controls me
I am a person who has lost the capability to trust
I have lost the capability to love
I am not a princess
I do not get a fairy tale ending
In the end no one will ever truly want someone
Who has been damaged beyond repair

Natalie McCallum
*Woodinville, WA*

## Serve Tomorrow

A chef follows a recipe,
Finds the ingredients and spices,
To ensure the dish turns out right.
She creates it to feed.
A good chef cooks with passion,
With her heart and soul,
So the dish becomes a representation of herself.
She creates it to deliver,
To feed, to provide, to serve.
The first chef does as told,
She abides by her recipe and bounds,
She settles for someone else's creation,
Rather than realizing her own.
A good chef wanders away from the kitchen,
And returns feeling inspired.
She wishes to experiment, to impress.
She discards the common recipe,
And builds her own that she will serve.
The first chef says goodbye to guests,
As she returns to clean,
And she prepares for another day.
The good chef stays at the dinner table,
Observing her guests and their tastes,
Inside her mind, she is taking notes,
Which she will serve tomorrow.

Sanjana Sinha
*Rancho Santa Margarita, CA*

## The Artist

With a speck of blood dripping down my crippled face,
I curl my toes, gripping the rusty iron poles that encloses me within an eerie capsule of accumulated fears,
A delightful aroma slithers into my chamber's creases,
Living ebony latex, it must be,
I prance my head slowly unsure of what this spirit will command of me.
Walk with me, come now, murmured this divine entity of mystique and determination,
Confused, I reply: but a scalpel to my leg, do you not remember?
What use will I be with a limping leg?
Veins begin protruding out of her arms,
And sweat secretes from her thin, patched fingers as she hesitates to approach my grotesque corpse scattered across the shadowed floor,
A sharp sensation ravaged so sporadically as she
skins my leg with the arrow of cupid and the blade of a demon,
Such an eloquent figure carving on my leg as she would a canvas!
A teardrop bounces off her regretful eye into my skin of crimson galore,
And dead I am proclaimed,
But free I am from the pain that I've endured.

Juaneduardo Lorenzo
*Miami, FL*

## The Truth Behind Our Eyes

Eyes are like snowflakes, no two pair are alike. We all have different
eyes, brown, blue, hazel, grey, green, Different sizes, shades, shapes.
Eyes can be a mystery, we can only see with our eyes not someone else's.
What we see is, not always what we think is accurate. While we can see
emotions in eyes, we don't always see the truth that is behind them.
I thought I always knew what was behind Julie's eyes. I thought I
could see past those charming, creamy, chocolate brown eyes. But
I was wrong. We were all wrong. The crinkle that the corner of her
eyes made when she smiled was a sham. Her eyes weren't filled with
laughter and happiness that I saw, instead they were filled with
melancholy and dissatisfaction. Behind her eyes stood walls of anxiety,
depression, and OCD. Behind her eyes was a mind repeating over and
over that she wasn't good enough, screaming loudly that she wasn't
perfect. With my eyes, I never saw the internal battle that Julie was
facing alone. With my eyes I only saw the mask Julie put on, covering
the truth behind her eyes.
Sometimes, it's different. Sometimes people want to let us in past their
eyes. Sometimes, they need a way to express their emotions without
words. They allow their eyes to be like whirlpools, luring us in, like
the smell of salt air when you walk along the beach, until our eyes are
trapped with no way of leaving. They want our eyes to see their pain
without them having to explain their past. They want our eyes to act
as wrecking balls, disassembling the barriers they have constructed
around their minds. They want us to see the agony and torture that
their minds have put them through. They desire us to taste our own
salty tears as they stream down our face stricken in sadness. They need
us to stare. Really stare into their eyes until we see them standing in
the middle of the fields of battle and war alone and vulnerable, waiting
for someone to reach out their hand to seize them from this recurring
nightmare that they have to live with. They need us, they need us to see
the truth behind their eyes.

Sophia Sanchez
*Stanhope, NJ*

*I am fifteen years old. My poem is about the truth behind our eyes. We think we know what's going on, but we can't really see it. I'd like to dedicate this poem to all who struggle with sharing their emotions and letting people into their mind.*

## Moth

This is Moth, surprised?
This is the hole of a bacteria, surprised?—Psych Professor
This is Lexapro, surprised?—M.D.
No, I was actually going to bring it up.
The fountain is down the hall
past the bathroom—people like to talk looking in the mirror.
The quick stop-n-chats are just as stale as the mold clinging to the carpet
lined with all of shellacked wood doors.
I used to like the riddle about two twins in front of two doors—
one was a good door, one was a bad door.
Ask questions of the twins—one is truthful, one lies.
"If I asked the other twin which door leads to heaven,
what would they choose?"
It was fun when there were two doors, and when I was twelve.
But even if just half of the doors are hell,
There are fifteen gates to hell on the way to the water fountain.
And half the time I say "what's up?"
You're lying when you say you're good.
And you'll go to hell; I hope it's with Milton's Satan.
Make me root for you.
I touch the tiny white pill to my tongue.
It slides off the sweat of my finger, clings to the dryness of my tongue.
I wait for my dad to make a joke about "hard to swallow pills,"
but he never does.

Gustie Owens
*New York, NY*

## Residues

I am the essence of leftover crumbs
From a dream not fully baked yet.
I am collecting the specks of
Glitter left behind, endlessly shining.
I am holding on to the feather
That was plucked from the dove
All those dreams ago
Without warning.
I am the essence of reaching up,
Trying to pick off the moon and
The stars, like stickers
From the vast blanket
Of the midnight breeze surrounding me.
I am the essence of residues
From a memory
I used to call home.

Maria Gil
*Lynbrook, NY*

## My Prepossessing Prisoner

Why do you insist on hindering your escape?
Hath thine intuition failed thy soft heart?
Causing your inevitable dejection?
I've warned you of my complications,
I shall cut you in your stability.
My falsehoods and customs stand to narcotize your dull mind.
To thrust my blood upon your canvas as a mask,
Your free ardor twined with my lovely knife.
I require your presence when I need my own
You do not perceive the true, lucid me.
Don't omit the other monster, yourself;
Neglect not your origin
Do not detest my creation,
The scars upon your mitts are to adhere.

Macarria Mitchell
Moultrie, GA

## Lost

I run with nowhere to go
I love with no feelings to show
I hide from my own soul
Because I'm too afraid to let myself grow
I stare at the mirror daily
Wish I could see the image clearer
But I only see it vaguely
I haven't been able to tell who I am lately
And it pains me greatly  How do I find a purpose?
How do I prove to myself that life is worth it?
How do I convince myself that I'm not worthless?
And smile through it all no matter how much I'm hurtin'
I have to go through this everyday
So lost but I'll never say
Don't worry about me I'll never complain
I'll push through it no matter how much I'm drained
Because that's just how life is
A puzzle with no prizes
We go through it with many surprises
Doesn't matter if we're delighted or frightened
We all go for the light in the end

Jorae Torres
*San Antonio, TX*

## My Missing Puzzle Piece

When I look at her,
I see this puzzle with missing pieces.
I see all her pieces floating around her
But she can't seem to put them in place,
Even the corner pieces.
I wonder if she's lost a side piece along the way.
Her edges are jagged and they don't quite fit
How they're supposed to.
Almost as if she took other pieces from other puzzles
And tried to make them fit flush.
But it doesn't work that way and she knows it.
The people in her puzzle are fragmented and fuzzy,
Almost as if she doesn't want to remember them.
I want to help her.
I want to find her corner pieces.
I want to find those missing sides.
I want to fix those fuzzy faces.
I can reach out and help put them back.
And maybe with a little time,
She can put my puzzle back together.

Kenzie Lanning
*Firestone, CO*

## Sharp Love

I'm sorry I took your life.
I'm sorry I cut you deeper this time.
I'm so sorry.
I'm sorry I fell to the floor
of the shower and broke in two.
I'm not as strong as I look.
I'm sorry I clattered against the porcelain sink,
your hands were too shaky to hold me.
I'm sorry I sat at the bottom of a drawer while you were away.
I would've gone with you, but you wanted to keep me safe.
I'm sorry I didn't hide fast enough when your mom
came to check in for dinner.
That I started a fight and made you cry.
If I knew that was the last time you'd hold me,
I might have wiped the tears from your face
before I kissed your wrists.
I'm sorry I took your life, as you were everything to me.
Your favorite color was red, and that's all I ever wanted to give you.

Lexie Gipson
*Goldsboro, NC*

## Nepenthe

The tablet on my tongue is tasteless,
And a cloud of smoke hits my face.
Powder is lined up on the table, weightless;
The syringe is filled with a murky orange, nameless.
Getting the highest is winning the race.
Scars reopened by life defining metal,
Burns scattered across my arm.
Starvation is the only thing I'll settle;
Scratching is the way I mettle.
Sometimes, no one is there to stop the harm.
Tequila is being poured into a shot glass,
While my friend smiles and says, "Vodka, instead."
Serving our drinks, there's a cup of gin—high class.
An ice cube swishes in a glass of whiskey—crass.
This alcohol is downed without dread.
Lust-filled eyes greet me at the door,
I know I want this, but I take five.
The look in his eyes tells me I'm a whore.
It's painful, but I ask for more.
And I know, these are the reasons I'm alive.

Kiarra Pamer
*Mogadore, OH*

*When I wrote "Nepenthe" I was a freshman in high school. I've always loved creative writing but the summer before high school was when I discovered my love for poetry. Nepenthe was not inspired by one specific topic but a few topics difficult to discuss. Personally, darker subject matter has always been the easiest to write about, but I write in a range of emotions.*

## Cauliflower Boy

Cauliflower boy.
Why do they laugh?
You are delicate, whiter than snow.
Difference is good, Cauliflower boy!
Yet he still hides away.
They'll live up to see!
Nobody did.
"Why me?"
He wonders aloud.
That Cauliflower boy, oh so alone.
Everything is damaged.
Walking in.
So ugly.
So sensitive and weak, yet pushing to victory.
That Cauliflower boy, once full of dread.
This chapter must not end just yet.

Chloe Wright
*Youngsville, LA*

## Yesterday Mourning

living these days through the haze of what is left.
My mother is gone, what is left?
Her love never was lost, always in my mind
With every breath, mother and son inter twined.
I think she was lost, feeling nothing but pain
She lost her loved ones, no blood left in her vein
I think she gave up, living in the past
Tears fall down
the heaviest of rains
Her ship has moved on..full mast
The ocean of life rocked her too hard
Now I'm the one left, emotionally scarred.
I pick up the phone, forget shes not there
The pain is creeping, feels like my ship is sinking
Horrors at night start seeping, no sleeping
Overthinking, analyzing, criticizing
Can I escape my own prying eyes
The most I can do is try to move on
But it's hard to do
When your mother is gone.

Samuel Smalley Jr.
*Dickinson, ND*

*This is for the people who have lost a loved one, but some things don't always sink in fast enough. Constantly picking up the phone or mentioning them. Some people see it as not accepting the truth. I see it as she will always be here in my mind. I love you mom and, yes, I still smile when I think of you. I'm still waiting for you to come haunt me like you promised. I miss our humor and long talks. Hugs and Eskimo kisses pretty little lady.*

## Strength

We read a book that said a hard thing
Strengths us
But what does it mean to be strong?
Does it mean to be a lion?
Strong never showing weakness?
Or is it to be a lamb?
Vulnerable and at times scared?
Or is it to be a tsunami?
Rushing in and destroying everything?
Or is it to be a flower?
Beautiful and sweet with a will to survive?
What does it mean to be strong?

Carlee Turner
*Powell Butte, OR*

*I wrote "Strength" while struggling with anxiety. The day I wrote it I was feeling really inspired and started to think about what it truly meant to be strong in this part of my life. My mom told me I was so strong almost every day and their encouragements inspired me to start asking questions about what it meant. In my free time I love riding and spending time with horses. I hope to have a future in writing and riding as a competitor or trainer.*

## The American Dream

Human beings glued to a radioactive screen
Disconnect and be unseen
Every last move is being analyzed
Only to be chopped, manipulated, and scrutinized
Artificial light stimulating and transmitting
Tricking the nerves and drugging the brain
As they lay asleep like infants
And the thought of their diabolic plan comforts them and helps them rest easy
Knowing that the world is slowly morphing into a state of unease
Elitist and hypocrites grinning in the dead of the night
While the masses are left paranoid and unsettled
Contemplating every last gesture
Tearing the hairs out trying to find the answers
It's all a set up
It's all a set up
Invade
Damage
Occupy
It's all a set up  Saturation overload
Stimulation instead of meditation
Disconnect and be unseen

Nicholas Shrestha
*Trabuco Canyon, CA*

*I am a student at the University of California Irvine studying English literature. In my free time I write and record music as well as write poems and short stories. Thanks for reading my poem.*

## Reflection

Five in the morning,
The wind is blowing
Tweedy birds singing.
Crawling out of bed,
Cold floor against my bare feet,
The cold air against my warm skin,
The roaring of an engine in the driveway,
Walked to the window in a hurry,
Watching the pickup disappear in the fog,
Out of nowhere I suddenly heard a bark of a dog,
Walked quietly to the bathroom,
Something caught the corner of my eye,
Breathing heavily
No longer stressed,
I feel relieved, safe,
Wanted, Calm,
Looking at my reflection through the clear mirror,
Looking at my long blond hair.
My bright blue eyes full of curiosity,
But all I could see is my flaws,
Why am I so tall,
Why are my ears so big,
Why are my teeth so yellow,
Why am I different,
Why can't I be pretty
I want to be popular,
I want to be noticed,
Why me
Why

Kristie Milner
*Christmas Valley, OR*

## Alternate Rapunzel

let's talk about it
your past
the things that make you, you I'll go first -
locked away in a tower of traumas
there is a story
about a princess who was controlled
through her hair
yes, you read that correctly
her hair
she was never allowed to have long hair;
strict orders from the king
she cried and wished
and imagined what it felt like to
have hair that touched her back
but she never got that chance
until the king moved away for good
so when people ask why I don't cut my hair
there's more to it than
"I just like it long"

Sarah Ciminillo
*Clarkston, MI*

*Hello! My name is Sarah Ciminillo and I'm twenty-three years old. Poetry has been such a huge part of my life since I was a young girl; it was, and still is, the way I express and deal with my emotions. What inspired this poem is what also inspired my passion to write in the first place - my father. Suffering from his emotional abuse blossomed into creativity and an everlasting love for poetry and writing.*

## Angels, Demons, and a Leftover

The door closed behind me
With a sharp, curious noise
I was looking bluntly
Actually, looking for nothing.

Conversations, simple, formal
Some cliched paperwork
I was feeling sleepy, kind of numb
Racing thoughts, awkward silence.

Window glasses, scattered raindrops,
An epic view of an off-peak outside world
Where, at night, the street lights create an illusion,
A very mystic dream of life.

Beautiful faces, smiling, inspiring
Through a gradual sense of solitude, loneliness.
In poems and prayers; in pieces of personal notes
In songs of angels, demons and a leftover.

Tamanna Ferdous
*Round Rock, TX*

## Imaginary Religion

They're busy praising
Empty idols and hollow gods
Pledging their undying allegiance to one and
Then the next
They shout and scream and
Act obscene
And expect to reap much
But unknowingly sow nothing.
They blindly worship the
Things they see
And follow the leader down
Paths of destruction
Yet no one notices.
Bandages cover their
Damaged eyes and
Even if their blood no longer
Needs to spill
They continue to split themselves open
Sacrifice everything
All that matters and exists
To a shell of nothing
Inspired by something
But ultimately meaningless
And they don't suspect a thing.

Jabrecia Washington
*McLeansville, NC*

## Deep

Thoughts are deep there's nothing I want to keep.
Time is lonely on this dark night as I look into sight.
Nothing comes to mind.
I know there is something to find.

Catherine Ewald
*Chadron, NE*

## Tightrope

Eyes like fresh honey glistening in the sun,
Yet piercing like the sting of a bee.
A laugh that sounds like keys of the ivory on a grand piano,
Yet sour of an untuned one.
The love that could conquer a million battles,
But swift like a blade piercing the heart.
A voice that of an angel
The one who'll carry me from my grave once this is over.
Movement like the wind on a spring day,
Threatening to transition to a tornado.
This love is dangerous but exciting,
Exactly like a tightrope.

Jocelynn Nicholson
*Beech Grove, IN*

## Why I Lie To My Therapist

A sand-land with dry heat and cacti dead with inky blue skies, flash-freezing the night. House plants watered to fill the hollow stead, baptized or engulfed in Cavite. I wanted to run to escape far away, only my mistake was looking back to see my family at a ****ed-up tea party. Cracked porcelain cups filled with dirty, warm well-water. The teddy bear to my right splits open my geode skull and carefully considers its nuances. Admires light dancing off Jasper edges, artfully chisels out the shards of red and sands over the rough edges, shows the world I'm kosher.

Shelby Sands
*Pontiac, MI*

## History

Grandpa used to have a band.
Oh, the stage is our dreamland.
Grandpa always played guitar,
both born to be a star.
Singing the songs of old country artists,
playing the rhythm that was once known.
My dream is running ahead of me,
strumming the strings of my history.

Madison Richmann
*Keenesburg, CO*

*I am fourteen years old and live in Keenesburg, CO. I wrote this poem about my great-grandpa who shared a love of music and performing with me. I turned this poem into a song and recorded it. When my grandpa passed, my song was played at his funeral. I have been writing poems/songs since kindergarten and hope to someday write a hit song.*

## Saku-san

What pleasure's mere good health, eh?
Thus speaks Saku-san: brutal
Elucidation of the futile state of our
Span. Especially in a funereal room,
A once sacred space (or, at the very least, enjoyed);
Now it reeks of the bedpan, anemic,
Void of what once was, of the merry-old,
Left to decline with the seasons,
Putrid, cold. Prevaricating, I exit the chasm to enter another:
Confused, despairing, chary to commit to this tangible
Phantasm, I flee to Sensei, or God, or some
Other force of reason. But what is reason on this spiraling
Sphere? Jumbled are the lyrics to humanity's air;
Cacophonous, we try to barter with the inevitable
But come up cozened. Christ,
I just want to make sense of this muck,
But who doesn't? So I reenter the chasm, look into my father's waning eyes,
Mouth slightly ajar, pale, defeated; and I
Give in to eternal recurrence, ouroboros, simply realizing
That we've been cheated.

Cameron Bennett
*Springfield, MA*

## Anxiety

Dread
Hope
I hear my name and the worst has happened
I need to be positive
My heart bursts
My heart goes faster than a race car
Everyone gets this feeling right?
My eyes see clearly but I don't see anything
I know I am equal, but I feel nothing
Am I walking funny?
Where should I put my hands?
Thoughts battling almost as much as my heart and chest
The same fear you get when a car is heading straight towards you
Everything is fine.
I am stronger than my fears
I can do this
I read my paper in front of the classroom.

Bri Parker
*North Attleboro, MA*

## My Son Is Addicted to Drugs

My son is addicted to dope
Please Jesus help me learn how to cope
He is Your precious child
Even if he is high and oh so wild
My husband and I love him so
Dear Jesus I wish You he did know
When I see him please tell me what to say
He needs to know that You are the only way
He needs to know the Father, Son and Holy Spirit
I want to tell him, but will he want to hear it
Please dear God, protect my son
And let me tell him about Jesus the Risen One
If only he knew to always turn to You
In everything he endeavors to do
In heart, Jesus, You must dwell
So he can live long enough to tell
Of how from drugs he was saved
And to crack, he had been so enslaved
To others he could proclaim You as his Savior
And in turn, do them a favor
Introduce them to Jesus, God's only Son
The One through whom Eternal Life is won

Patricia Monroe
*Youngstown, NY*

## Balance

I don't know why,
I just feel like I'm pained.
I guess it's just one of those days.
Like everything is going wrong,
Yet nothing has changed.
That's the crazy thing,
In tuned with spirits but can't hear the Angels sing.
The light just blinds my eyes,
But a cool breeze is what the darkness brings.
Stuck inside a vessel with wandering eyes.
A soul wanting to savor each moment but sever all ties.
A constant battle in which I,
The enemy lies.
But can you really win,
If a part of you dies?
They say it's for the better.
Was it institutionalized?
The evil is misunderstood,
It even burns itself when it cries.
Without the dark half of my wings,
Tell me how do I fly?
Please tell me,
Without the negatives,
How does the positive thrive?

Aaron Hooper Jr.
*Bronx, NY*

## Hum

A hum breaks the silence. It turns peace into unease.
A single trembling note, and then it fades.
Not lasting long enough to gain reason or tune.
Forcing the senses into a heightened awareness. An upset angst.
A man sits alone. Staring at the ground. Unaware of the fear he causes.
Every hum is another word to this spell of destruction.
Each half note, like scissors to a nerve. Dissonant. Unpleasant.
A sound that should be pleasant, used so wrong.
Be afraid.
White noise is not strong enough to fight this.
The screams inside your mind cannot drown it out.
Run down the corridor, leaving everything behind.
Find safety. The sound is gone, locked away in that room.
But the musicless note follows you, and stays in your mind.
Growling. Prowling.
In movies, it is exactly this sort of hum that is used to portray insanity,
as a man with hands in pockets, strolls down a corridor.
Afraid of the mind that could produce such a sound,
but is it rightly so?
Fear, wrapped in unease.
And so we hide, until the sound abates.

Rowan Oliver
*East Falmouth, MA*

## To the Lord of Green

O sing to thee, a cherished Lord of Green.
Let none of the others go far to see.
Disasters befall those who intervene.
Grace, help good men's safety guarantee!
Thy life's thread is not meant to be broken.
Thy wish is a command. Harm is taken.
What thou desire needs fetched a token.
O Lord of Green, let the times be making.'
All swords' reign has settled, but guns still storm.
The sun resigns its comfortable sky,
While fires a-blaze, passing the clock's form.
The strongest force has no wish to comply.
A soldier's heart is heavy, passes the time.
Not won, but two sides still fight for their lives.
For someone they hold dear, not for a dime.
O Lord of Green, spare them who love their wives.
It's true that love shall come and come to pass.
Just know, thy fight for love will ever last.

Meredith Marks
*Williamsburg, VA*

## End of the Beginning

I'll crawl out of the darkness and into the light,
To let the angels see me for once a beautiful sight.
I reach up above to bring down the ones that I love,
As I'm at peace with the world,
and I'm friends with the dove.
The air is calm, and the butterfly brushes my cheek,
My heart is stronger and stainless and no longer weak.
The air brushes through my hair as if it were my friend
I've made it to the beautiful palace, some call it,
The End
I'll remember the ones that I loved which who returned
The touch,
My eyes are like rain, with each drop is filled with
Sorrow to pain, am I asking too much?
Each seed grows with a new breath
of life a new beginning,
The rosey cheeks of a first look at
the world, and a start
Of the sinning.
The angels grin, and they see
The soul of one day an angel to be,
When one does the breath of a new life
Comes in and opens the eyes to see.
Open the clouds and let the rain fall
on me and caress my skin,
Cause I need to find the pathway to the endless maze within.

Kaylee Frye
*Westlake, LA*

## One More Day

I hide this all behind a smile
Hung my tears to dry awhile
So I kept holding on for one more day
I tried to see the bright side
But the good in things I could not find
But I kept holding on for one more day
I wanted not to care what people thought of me
But everything they said felt like
I was on strings
The flame inside of me I felt
I tried to put it out
Duct tape my heart back but how
I go to bed dreading the sunrise
And it seems like all I say are lies
But I kept holding on for one more day
I remember looking out
Thinking it would be so easy...
And I said no this won't end now
But now I can't hide behind a smile
My tears are done drying awhile
And I don't know if I can hold on for one more day

Kayla Baxter
*Lake St. Louis, MO*

## God Is with Us at All Times

Along the west bank,
the headlights speed up away.
We are flying, in the air with a happy smile
that keep us very happy in our life.

Now not one of those stars will kill
the heavy emerald of the water's wave.
We shall live in transparent Petropolis
where Persephone reigns over us.

We drink with every breath of life
and every hour may be our last.
The God that made the sea for us,
don't move your mighty helmet of stone.
In transparent Petropolis we shall live,
where life rules, is happy times for you.

I can sleep. All night long without getting up
to go to rest room.
I could list of all the things only to be happy:
the long-long way, the train of flying in the air
had lifted once the ancient Greece above.

I can sleep with a happy smile on my face
the time is now for us to be the kind of people-
that keep everyone very happy with in love
where do you go to have everything go your way in life.

Jerry Wells
*Los Angeles, CA*

*The Lord is within us all that have God's spirit. God's spirit lives in the light. The Lord is there in times of need as we pray to God for understanding the things that happen in our life so God can help us get through them.*

## Earth's Wounds

The Earth that is our home is in pain
And we humans are all the blame
Repeatedly stabbing its skin for treasure
Our greedy selves ripping its insides for leisure
The time has come to pay our fees
For destroying our lands we got for free
And now the clock is ticking
Waiting too long will be devastating
Death and destruction from floods and fire
Will bring fighting and famine making this dire
So why must we wait, deny, and bicker?
When knowledge and action is the real kicker!
So now we must all be doctors
Perform Earth's surgery for our sons and daughters
So they can live on and push for peace
Knowing that we can pass worrying the least.

Grant Martin
*Roseville, CA*

*I'll start with a fun fact, I hated English in highschool and thought I'd never use anything I was being taught. Well ironically two years after graduation, I striving to become a great poet and author! The two catalysts for me writing were my struggles with depression and loneliness in high school, as that was what my first poem was about, and my mom, as she's encouraged me and been my biggest fan of my writing since then!*

## Visions of Home

Cupboard full of half empty spice jars
Cabinets scattered with novelty salt shakers
Always something warm for the taking
Coffee table piled with National Geographic magazines
Alphabetized shelf of DVDs I can quote from memory
Always some quiet tune in the air
Murals on the walls everyone helped to paint
A steadily increasing collection of coin jars
All the security we needed
I will create a home for stray cats and stray friends
Make our lives in the style of midnight doughnut runs
And falling asleep during movies
My house will be a sanctuary for the people like me:
Drifting, seeking, wronged and powerful
Here, they will sleep soundly and wake up refreshed

Melissa Hayden
*Franklinville, NY*

*My name is Melissa and I'm a music education / creative writing student at the University of Arkansas. I grew up in a less than optimal household, and this poem is about building the future you needed in the past.*

## A Single Poem

A soliloquy of sorts, but in the form of a rhyme.
A play on words, told for the first time.
I, me, and my, is what it's all about.
A non-stop solo act, is what I'm pointing out.
"Just one?" is what I'm asked, "One please" is what I stated.
The restaurant staff would never say "Just two?" So now I'm irritated!
I'm expected to visit family at their homes, yet no one comes to see me.
Is it because I'm single? And have so much time that's free?
Why don't hotels in tony towns offer rooms with two separate beds?
It's because they prefer duos in a king or queen
So they only have to wash one bedspread.
Couples tend to pose with other twosomes,
So they can post their photos to the web.
When was the last time they took a photo with me?
Oh, that's right, odd numbers could disrupt the balance and ebb.
I'm expected to work late,
But not my partnered chums.
They tend to bolt out the door at 5 o'clock,
All because they're Dads and Mums.
This ode to being stag,
Probably sounds like a jaded tattle.
Whether going it alone or times two,
It's truly a constant battle!

Nuala Purcell
*Yonkers, NY*

*I am a freelance photographer in the New York area. Both of my parents are immigrants from Ireland and I was raised in the Woodlawn section of the Bronx. Irish people are known for the gift of lore, so I jokingly say I inherit the ability to come up with corny poems that almost always rhyme from my mother. I'm thrilled that a single poem of mine was selected as a semi-finalist. I penned a few observations I've made over the years as a single person living in a very coupled society.*

## Reveal

I took off my masks,
Revealing myself to you,
Only to be swallowed,
By the society lying within.

Emma Lund
*Sidney, MT*

## If You Ever Wonder How I Feel

I look upon you and see a whole universe for me to explore. When I hold your face in my hand, I hold galaxies. I've only explored what everyone can see but I want more. Let me trace your hands on your body to explore this new universe. I wanna know it like I know the back of my hand.  I am nothing but a person. A ruler of my own mind. The only thing I truly own is me. Whilst you rule over galaxies and millions of stars. I want to be part of one. I would like to play a part in one of your galaxies. And you can command me anyway or anyhow. You can make me bend to your will. Love me so. Love me dearly. And hold me tight in your arms and whispers the three words I long to hear. Give me your love so I may give it back twice as much. Embrace me. Love me. And care for me. So I say, again, and once more only. I love you. Your universe is as I am a person. But love me equally. Love me so.

Yasmin Campos
*Hondo, TX*

## Thinking of You

Do you think of me
I think of you
I dream of you
I even breathe of you
It's sick
I'm sick of you
Everything of you
I see you
Memories of you
I am of you
Mirrored image of you
Traces of you in my smile
Phrases of you
I used
We used
I constantly speak of you
Of us
I even laugh of you
Like you
Soft chuckles
About the good times
Sometimes I cry
Heavy sobs
About the bad times
I need to recover
But I'll always love you

Mylisha Phillips
*Marysville, WA*

## Disappointment

I try
Give everything
All I can do
But I still fail
I still disappoint you
All of you
You don't have to say it
Yet some of you do
I already know
What I am
How you feel
What you see me as
I'm the disappointment
Not smart enough
Tough enough
Good enough
I'm just the one you all hate
I'm your disappointment
The odd one out in the family
Forever
I will always be
A disappointment

Siri Deuel
*Welches, OR*

## Wasted Away

All the time I did nothing wasted away
I was like a drone
Doing what I was told
No freedom
No thoughts
No opinions
Just forced
Doing what I did not want to do
Wanting to escape
But I couldn't
Finally I had a way out
But I felt pressure
As if I was drawn to stay
Brainwashed
I wanted to leave more than anything
But all I felt was guilt
But yet, I knew years were wasted away
So why would I want to waste more?
Pressure
That is all I feel
I feel like I have to stay
I am not allowed to be anything but a drone
I can not make my own choices
But once I have a way out
A way out of abuse
I have nowhere to go
I feel like I must go back
To every day abuse

Ashley Ramsey
*Bartlesville, OK*

## A Letter to My Younger Self

Your eyes are from earth brown like the soil
You don't need them to be green, blue or grey to be beautiful
Matter fact your eyes are brown like soil and that what makes flowers bloom
You're the lotus that bloomed
The lotus that bloomed in a dark room
The room we call poverty, you ain't rich but your soul is and that's all that matters
Your skin is brown too, with a hint of honey
You don't need to be lighter boo, turn off that TV telling you YOU need to be lighter boo
Your hair twirls like DNA it grows to the sky
your hair resembles the trees which touches the sky
Your lips two different shades and that's beautiful too
Your nose resembles the pyramids you are beyond this planet little black girl watching TV thinking how to be pretty
You come straight from the earth you are pretty
You don't need to search how to be lighter or how to get "pretty eyes"
You're beautiful already
Your eyes come from soil and that what makes flowers bloom

Micaela Coleman
*Irvington, NJ*

*We live in a world of advanced technology and media. Someone is always trying to sell something so they use "beauty" to sell their product. However the meaning of beauty has been exploited and this causes insecurities in little boys and girls all over the world. At only seven years old I discovered self-hatred. I was a little girl in her small NYC apartment wondering why the girls on TV and in magazines don't look like me. I'm not fair-skinned, my hair coils, and my eyes aren't blue or green. But the things I'm not are being fetishized and displayed as the most beautiful. At sixteen years old I discovered self-love; my thoughts were rambling. I decide to take pen to paper and write a letter to the seven year old girl in that small NYC apartment. My poem isn't for that little girl only; it's for the little boys and girls, women and men who grew up like me—poor and lost, however, beautiful from the core to the surface.*

## Through the Looking Glass

Why didn't you tell me?
To run, to hide, to breathe
To fill my lungs with thick, black smoke
Choking on my last breaths
I'm free. Free at last.

You insult me. Poke at every last dignity I have.
I smile, pretend like nothing is wrong
Smack! You strike me in my prime.
Hoping not too look up at your eyes.
To see the envy of what happiness lies;
Behind the broken glass

Breathe. 5. 4. 3. 2. 1
I snap out of the trance
I'm home. Safe, secure, free
Exhale. Breathe

Maria Lawrence
*North English, IA*

## For the Longing

Hell on earth, of dreams, the rushing of all
Ostensible the making of confessions, a trio.
Levants that pilgrims must travel, to improv
Even the word, which is left, but raw to me.

Michael Virgl
*Channahon, IL*

## From Your First Breath to Your Last

Your life like a flower on the first day of spring
You grow, and you talk, and you play, and you sing
Life is as fresh as a summer's day
It feels like the heat will forever stay
But as time flies the leaves will all fall
A carpet of white will cover them all
The memories of summer pile up with the snow
And all you want is for winter to go
Winters almost over now and your heart grows cold
Longing for the warmth that has now grown old
The snow has gone and taken you with it
But spring will come again and new flowers will bloom

Ella Lallier
*Franklin, MA*

## Important

I'm not important
No one would care if I left
They tell me be gone
They tell me to disappear...
Why am I still here?
Who said I want to be here
Please stop assuming
I wish to be here right now
I know you don't care
But lucky you I'll be gone
I won't stick around
Tomorrow is my last day
The day to end it
And to those who claimed to care
I saw through your lies
So please don't concern yourself
With me any longer
I will make your wishes true...

Josh Ramos
*Windsor, CO*

## Not Alone

The dark is growing
The wind is whistling
People not knowing
But I am not alone

Birds not chirping
Spirits not whirling
Still people not knowing
But I am not alone

People teasing
Laughing, wheezing
Them not knowing
But I am not alone

Walls closing in
I cannot win
Again still people not knowing
But I am not alone

Nickole Robinson
*Las Vegas, NV*

## Can You Hear Me

Listen to me child  I hear you  can you hear me?
Come down from there  come down  Please
You don't recognize my voice?  I'll come closer
Over here  now can you hear me
This is not something child you really wanna do

Social Media  Cyber Bullying  Sexual abuse
Has seized many teens  many lives  such as you
Remove that cord  please  from around your neck
Don't you kick that stool  please  take a deep breath
Allow me to be the father you never knew

Please don't Jump child  Move away from the Edge
Suicide is not the answer  Look at me  Take my Hand
You've made the right Decision  Not taking your Life
It's Okay to Let Go  You are Almost There
I'll Catch You  I Promise I Won't Let-go  I Love You

Emily Mathis
*Fort Worth, TX*

*Emily is the widow of a Vietnam veteran Frank W. Mathis Jr. who served twenty-two years in USAF. Frank was paralyzed from the neck down the last six years of his life. Single-handedly as caregiver, writing novels and poetry became therapy for the writer. "Can You Hear Me" was inspired by the increase in teen suicide. Emily hopes if one teen reads this poem they will know they are loved by the Creator of the universe.*

## They

What did they expect me to do? When they kept pushing me.
They think they have me, but, I'll always be free. Freer than thee.
They can take my thoughts and twist it into truth or dare.
But beware; kindness turns to anger. Shame turns into pride. They're causing me to snap. Cause, this is the fact. They pushed me way too far. Off the point of keeping reality into check and not without cursing the ones whom started this bet.
They should have known by what my human nature could tell that "touching," " tasting," "smelling," "seeing" and "hearing" had all been corrupted, I for one have had enough of it. Unknowingly, playing the part of a self-sabotage mission inside of my mind. Hundreds are battling but yet looking in the mirror that hangs all I see is a one-on-one battle. It leaves an imprinted rattle from deep deep within. The memory makes an unbearable turmoil and the scars left behind is a reminder of what lingers. They cannot take my heart for the loved one's are kept there. Those of whom that begin to look there will see that no fear can be here. "Blessings" from our heavenly father also belong here. They can torture me and others around me will see a very different part of me. For whom myself I did not want to see, or maybe I have become blind by the silence. Yet knowing, that I have not the patience nor the silence. Being bullied and becoming bruised everyday. Boundary lines have been crossed. I broke myself. So let them know when I go, that my love was pure. Going to hell and back was endured. I don't know how I got here. I know that I do not want to stop to stare anywhere. I just want out of here. And so now where are they?

Lauren Hicks
*Corpus Christi, TX*

## Untitled

Young brown girl
The one with tear-filled eyes
but with the
blaze of a thousand suns.
They cannot hold you down.
Yes, they may throw stones,
crucify your name.
And spit at the sight
of your proud walk.
But they cannot hold you down.
You have embodied
Kali
to conquer the worlds,
including your own,
to resurrect your
once lost soul.
You are divine.
You are a goddess.
Oh, young brown girl.
You are the universe
personified.

Pooja Raj
*Astoria, NY*

## My Life as a Hallmark Movie

Sitting on my couch,
binging on cheap chocolate and expensive red wine,
I scroll through my options,
return to what I know:
A 3 ½ star rated movie on Netflix that is placed under some obscure genre title like "strong female lead in an indie Rom-com flick."
I've seen it before, but I'll watch it again to get a good laugh at my life.
Condensed into only 93 minutes,
the lead romantic interest changes quickly and often,
while the lead is never settled; not in a city, home, relationship, or clique, wistfully moving and leaving, always saying goodbye.
I'll laugh and cry with this character I'm deeply connected to and wonder:
Who writes this shit? This doesn't happen in real life!
But the end is always a cliff hanger,
wondering what situation she'll fall into next.
Netflix will ask me:
"Are you still watching?"
"Why are you still watching?"
click continue,
play from beginning.

Adare Toral
*San Luis Obispo, CA*

## The Message

I carved your name upon my wrist
In hopes it'd make you stay
But you took one look and that was it
You went your separate way
Now I'm left with doubts and regrets
More pain than I could stand
So I let your name fade slowly
And then I carved it on my hand
This time it was different
It was not to keep you here
It was now a physical reminder
Of the cross that I must bear
I'll let this pain overtake me
I'll let it dim my light
Because now instead of being happy
Its everyday I fight

Jessica Rice
*Siloam Springs, AR*

## My Love?

I sit in my room and ponder my life's journey.
Where am I going? Who am I going with?
I find myself alone in the dark. Why doesn't she love me?
My world spinning out of control with no room to breathe.
Why do they disrespect me so?
Have I not provided with the little I get? I wonder, will my worries end?
I am not happy nor am I suicidal.
Stuck somewhere in the middle
Like the man in between a rock and a hard place.
Why do I suffer so? I wish she wanted me.
I am never protected yet I am the protector.
She's never had my back. Why do I feel like a child?
Helpless, secluded, alone.
No partner in crime, no one to hear my pleas for escape.
I want to run away,
But there are responsibilities I have committed to.
He has my heart.
The moment I laid eyes on him; I knew he was a fighter.
I knew he was going to be my wing-man.
Why is he so sickly?
All the time; nonstop with the sickness that never goes away.
I'm trapped. I can't concentrate.
Like a slave, I take care of him with no reward from her.
She never wanted me. I should leave. I should go far away.
Why am I stuck on her? Too many thoughts, not enough action.
I should leave. I will leave. I am gone.

Martin Otero
*Elmhurst, NY*

## Heal My Soul

He has always been there
Always been by my side
He's always held my hand
Been my shoulder when I cry
Now I just don't know, I don't know what to do
I go to my knees, God I pray to you

Help with the brokenness
The tears that I cry
Help with the loneliness and the struggles in my life
Help me God, I just need you
Heal my soul
Tell me the reasons he had to go

Does it get any better, do I cry less each night
Life without him just doesn't seem right
Will I always hurt or will the pain ever ease
I ask you God will you help me please

Help with the sadness that's down in my soul
He was the kind of man you can't forget or let go
Help me God, please help me, I just need you
Heal my soul
And tell me the reasons he had to go

Amy Hale
*Hohenwald, TN*

## A Reason to Be

Alone, surrounded by people.
Looking for meaning amongst the stars.
Destined to never raise above the Earth.
Is there a reason to be?
Is there a reason to be me?
Never have I belonged.
Yet, many count on me.
Would they fall if I were gone?
Would they fly without me by?
Happiness is an elusive dream.
Is there a reason to be?
Is there a reason to be me?
Forever roaming, never finding the answer.
Will I fly?
Will I soar?
More and more it seems like no.
No reason for me.

Shawn Ellison
*Onsted, MI*

## You Were Not My Intention

You make precise decisions on what you say to me while planning our
hellos and good-byes at the same time.
You make me want you enough to stay, but hate you enough to leave.
Empty conversations filled with lies and small talk leave me wanting to
shred the transcript my mind has recorded.
After talking I feel like nothing has been accomplished and more
problems arise.
I can't call it a mistake if it's a mistake I choose to make, at that point
it's a decision.
I board myself up for days and turn out the lights because I'd rather be
in the solitude of darkness then have to openly mourn just the thought
of you.
It's as if you've vanished because I let you have a part of me and now I
don't matter enough, nor have I ever.
You were a light pillar of hope that gleamed at dusk but I hit the rocks
anyway.

Jenna Hahn
*Oak Harbor, WA*

## The Feeding

What have you fed yourself of late?
What information is on your plate?
Tabloids, cat videos, laughing babies too
Pinterest, Etsy or online payments due

Scrolling luminescent blue light
Blinding ourselves late at night
You should be sleeping in your bed
What mindless waste do you imbibe instead?

What themes crawl across your feed?
Politics, news stories, updates to read
Births, weddings, an acquired degree
Histrionic posts for the world to see

Our minds slowly crumbling to dust
Our poor posture and joints turning to rust
Instant gratification at its very best
Attention spans no longer put to the test

Inert bodies, mindless and numb
Years pass, scrolling with one thumb
Icarus flew close and never turned
Just like him, we too may get burned

Linnea Kellar
*Eastport, MI*

## Heritage Frontier

I heard our ancestors came on the May Flower boat
Sad part there wasn't a journal or note
It's a miracle Thomas and Susan landed on Plymouth rock
A vision of their voyage made me feel a shock
Its futile to prove when our first ancestors got here
The government kept us from making history so dear
Our pilgrims survived the rough sea
And this legacy means something to me
Our first pilgrims died on Plymouth rock somewhere
Our kins migrated to Virginia and Tennessee from there
Our lineage was kept in a bible like a passport
Our freedom was stronger from England's deport
My pilgrim learned from natives how to grow food
The natives didn't think our over population was good
The natives didn't have concept of owning land
Everything was stolen by the white man

Jennifer Spase
*San Antonio, TX*

*Learning about my ancestry is very deep. It took a lot of study to tap into self-discovery in what makes me unique. My identity doesn't have a title for our long heritage other than we call ourselves original Americans. I do consider myself a unique native with non-tribal status. I believe the revolutions have destroyed part of my family identity. Our history has been glossed over by half truths. There's a lot of unseen stuff and mystery how we white settlers came to America. We do believe we had a purpose to be in America. The earliest white Americans were welcomed here in America. The natives had no concept of owning land. There was peace for ten years until the whites over-populated the natives. There was much revolution and genocide with native who didn't want to share the land. The natives were condemned for not being Christian and moved to trail of tears in 1830.*

## Lights

Tim opened a light fixture store
It opened when I was eight.
He sold lanterns, bulbs, and lamps
I thought it was pretty great.
The building was kind of rusty,
His marketing was a bit cheesy,
His slogan was: Lights make you happy!
So happiness sounded easy.
But I was not easily happy,
I was more sad than my parents knew.
So I headed off to Mr. Tim,
He will know what to do!
He said: "Howdy there little one!"
"What can I do ya for?"
I told him I was unhappy
And life had become a bore
I asked him what was feeling.
This dark thing that wouldn't cease.
"Your job is selling lights!"
"This is your area of expertise!"
His smile faded away.
And on his chair I sat.
He said: "I wish I had better news..."
"But I don't sell lights for that."

Gabrielle Blake
*Titusville, FL*

## What I Love Most

What I love most is not but one object.
It is that ethereal ocean's flow;
It is that bright and shining white of snow;
It is that blend of forest, realm o' sprites;
It is that tiny hill, both small and slight;
It is that crescent moon's curve, oh so prime;
It is that song o' birds, oh so sublime;
It is that constellation on vast space;
It is that sound of life, that which, you brace;
Who I love most is truly one subject.

Pedro Avalos Jimenez
*Barrington, IL*

## Such Is Life

This world is a crazy place so you gotta keep up with the pace. Always make sure you have that one friend who will stick with you to the end. Family is a blessing from above to cherish and love. So, keep them close because they are the ones you need the most. But, on the other hand, don't just trust anyone because you will regret that relationship when it's done. Make God a staple in your life because without Him, nothing seems right. These are just a few life lessons that overtime you will learn so that your life is of no one else's concern.

Chelsea A. Hoffner
*Dover, DE*

## Special Love

This story describes love
That I saw and felt
Never seen anything like this
Because maybe it is a spell
Every time they meet, there is something special
See it in their eyes
How much they love each other
Nothing can come between them
They have a special bond
It holds them together
For life and beyond

Khadija Umer
*Upper Darby, PA*

## Vent

No peace of mind can't seem to breathe
Just like a planted flower being choked out by a weed
God help me please I'm in distress and dire need
My light is getting dim and not much more blood I can afford to bleed
I'm on my knees, escape is what I'm trying to achieve
My body is getting cold and heart is missing beats
I'm feeling weak.
Just trying to VENT cause I want to get some sleep

Samuel Cameron
*Scranton, SC*

## Wrath

This world is consumed of me.
I take pride in my achievements.
The internal feeling,
when I see myself in those black eyes,
is priceless,
Intoxicating.
My owner's neighbor had an opinion of me,
Tsk Tsk, not a good idea.
Our friend stole money from us,
Tsk Tsk, he will regret it.
Our wife betrayed us,
Tsk Tsk, she will pay.
World War II, the Holocaust,
The Oklahoma City bombing,
Nine Eleven,
Douglas school shooting.
Slavery, murder and torture
I have been there for all and much much more.
Proud and fulfilled,
I am winning.

Vanessa Rodriguez
*Chicopee, MA*

*My first time writing a poem was at age sixteen. I remember the title, "I Am English Like the Queen of England." The teachers liked it so much they published it along with other poems they were making for a project. It was surprising because I didn't really try to make a good poem. I just wrote. So I continued to write. And my inspiration for this poem "Wrath" isn't any different from my other poems. So I leave you with this: Life is nothing more than just hard and evil. Although it may be at times beautiful, its beauty fades very quickly. Us humans, regardless of what we've gone through and have done, are still here as survivors, victims, and even monsters. It is too bad we are the reason why life and this planet is suffering. So I write, I guess, to distract myself from what's around me, just for a few moments.*

## To My Brothers

Once we were alive and young in a summer
that was as new and naïve as us. Thinking
we walked where none had walked before, ruled
in secret spaces between brush and brambles. In a
kingdom keeping hours from dusk to dawn we ran
and screamed and shouted — until we had banished the
threats that lurked at the periphery of our imaginations —
specters that by day would be stark and boring reflections of our lives.
The stars remember the secrets we told them, even if one day we
do not. Forget the smell of wet grass between bare toes or
the pride of bloodied hands full of berries or a sun that
burned our skin as surely as our hearts burned with
the importance of the innocent — undeserving
but unashamed to see in the world what
we wished — and nothing more.

Megan Organist
*Jefferson Hils, PA*

## Give Your Mother Peace

Breathe deeply
And release
Enough with the strife
Enjoy your life
Upon the love of others, you will rise
Open your heart and let go of lies
Surround yourself with others who do the same
Don't waste time placing blame
The truth is yours to find and face
Don't feel shame or disgrace
Or anything else they want you to
Just be you
Learn how to make your love increase
Give your mother peace-

Dylan Duckworth
*Sullivans Island, SC*

## Dreaming

Dreaming, in all my dreaming
I see everything so clearly
For now it's all an illusion
Seems so far from reality
You say your faith in love is gone
But is it really gone forever?
The answer seems to be clear
Though at times I truly wonder
Dreaming, in all my dreaming
It's all clear to me now
I fear you see right through me
I just can't hide it somehow

Brad Berreman
*New Brighton, MN*

## Untitled

Overseen and understood,
Apocalypse of the mind,
Creativity at your fingertips,
You're one of a kind,
In a sweet sense of clarity,
You're on my mind,
I climb out the window in your arms,
And let the past fall behind,
I see green I see red I see blue,
And all the colors they're reminding me of you,
I see red I see red I see you,
But the blues inside of me it keeps me cool,
Keep a cool head, now I'm in a cool bed,
You played me for a fool, I'm a tool in your tool-shed,
Can't get a word in, edge wise,
So I say it all with my dead eyes,
Break apart then we put each other back together,
A million different ways and each and every one is ever better,
We did what we came here for,
And as I look back at you from the bedroom door,
You're attention gets me high now,
I'm living in the sky now,
I'm loving in the bed of the Angels,
In the cradle of your eyes.

Noa Thomas
*Monmouth, OR*

## Bass Guitar

The notes of Josh's bass guitar
hum through my body, a gentle earthquake.
Lavender incense fills every breath,
and I become calmer and calmer.
The melody brings me back
to when I was a little girl
with my dad, listening to the Alternative rock station
taking me to get a creamy Hershey's bar.
Now, as Josh is playing his bass guitar, with such passion
his emerald eyes lift from the strings and meet mine.
My open ears.
His magic fingers that could go on for days.
Music that fills the hot room is like water filling a deep cold swimming
pool.
We both get in to get out of the heat.
Never wanting to get out.

Tazesha Wilson
*Salem, OR*

## A Star's Lament

The sky will cry with her lament,
Her twinkling teardrops fall on me;
She screams and cries of her torment,
The sky will cry with her lament;
A breech of trust, vicious intent,
How could the world not hear her plea?
The sky will cry with her lament,
Her twinkling teardrops fall on me.

Jewel Medel
*San Antonio, TX*

## Corridors of My Mind

Welcome to the corridors of my mind.
Sit, right down and see what you find.
Better than gold to mind
Yes, the corridors in my mind.
Left, Right , Up, Down
You never know,
I guess you'll be fine

Nick Bukur
*Valparaiso, IN*

*Well I'll tell you I'm just a hard working guy with a wonderful family. I'm currently remodeling a house from inside out with the help from my wonderful wife Rhonda. I'm also writing a story about the house with the help of my two little turtle friends Thelma and Louie. These two characters are telling you the story of the house. The poem is like the book. It's about what your mind can do if; you put your mind to it. It's better than gold.*

## No, It Is Not a Sinking Feeling

my heart is not a ship
it is not sinking
sinking implies
that it was once something worth saving.
my heart is drowning
in the depths of the ocean,
where my lungs collapse,
into fossils of tortured history.
it is shattering
under the weight of tsunamis
that feed on
the often-ignored fragility of life.
it is crumbling
into something ugly and inhuman
yet all so familiar
to the human race.
so stop telling me
that all i need to do
is to raise my hand high
for someone to rescue me. . .
there is no me.

Oxlip Lam
*Cambridge, MA*

## Under the Stars

All alone
Under the stars
They shimmer and sparkle
Beauty like a diamond
Or the finest crown jewel
A light in the dark mystery
Purity in the black expanse
All unified but unique
Scattered and yet organized
Bright distant treasures
Each given a name
And lovingly noticed
But not me
Under the stars
All alone

Lauren Allen
*Fairfax, VA*

## Rays

Is the light here to stay?
Will it shine its amber rays?
An outstretched hand doth reach in haste
it craves those fleeting glory waves
But light is not found in the dark abyss
that encompasses the human consciousness
So struggle as you may young lass
with those yearning outstretched hands
And illuminate your dreary night
to rid your mind of its plight
However short lived it might be
relish in the opportunity
For in this black, decaying place
how precious are those peeking rays

Emma Winget
*Fairfield, CT*

## Moving On

You don't have to say I love you for someone to know
You think someone means it just because they say it, no
I've tried all my life to find out what love means
I thought it was easy, but trust me, it's a lot harder than it seems
God gave me the gift, he gave me the ability to write
But that's hard to do when you've lost your sight
I'm not talking about my literal eyes
I lost the ability to see a future without my demise
I see a broken man, with one too many bandages
When you pray for strength, God will give you challenges
You have to overcome them in order to become strong
I thought I had strength, but it turns out I was weak all along
I'm nothing without you Lord, and that's what really scares me
I sacrifice myself for others all the time, because it's my own worth
that I can't see
It's easy to pretend to be something you'll never be
When I look back at it now, it's actually pretty funny
I look in the mirror and laugh at myself
Did I think they would remember me as a friend or as something else
Maybe a hero, someone admirable
But then I realize that word is unfathomable
Because you can never give what you don't have
Maybe that's why no one around me can find happiness or a reason
to laugh
I've been searching for a reason to even exist
I hope someone relates to the heart I put in this
Been alone my whole life, but not by choice
God's the only one that's ever heard my true voice
My fiancée left me for a person I called friend
If my life were a book, after that, it'd say The End

Samson Lee
*Pembroke Pines, FL*

## No Connection

My soul visits a movie theater each day,
to watch my disjointed body sway.
My body has a mind of its own,
my mind bare, thoughts are in monotone.
My limbs are frail, barely holding on.
My will to live, slowly gone.
The last bit of hope that lies within,
Searching for a connection.

Julia Houghton
*Hanover, MA*

## My Journey

Traveling to vast lands
Fighting with a broken hand
Climbing the trees
To get away from the bees
Feeling the wind in my hair
Running away from a bear
Having to eat a snake
And bathe in a dirty lake
I finally finished my journey
It made me super weary
But I did gain something from this experience
The key to life is having patience

Abdurrahman Shahid
*New York City, NY*

## After You

I eventually found myself in truth. I think about my own sometime; a willowy pattern in darkness, for a battle of wits. Of unspeakable wisdom, adversity. There was spiritual work to do. I cannot let go of the energies invested in what I believed about you and what happened to you. I stood unafraid as we discuss supreme paradigm, holding natural delicacies long lasting lost touch with its tulle and effluvias style. Pull him up to the steps in a real authority as a familiar man, I as a young woman getting the best within itself in the shadows of what I understood to be a meaning of life. Time was odious as it proved as it enveloped eyes that would never see the beneficence of prevailing minds, of which I have no wealth. Brown eyed, when these two had lost touch with their commitment as I forged forward towards no regrets. The components of anti-trust in the depth of its conviction was torn from its form, to avoid an expensive paradigm.

Stephanie Pierce
*Alhambra, CA*

*"After You" is a poem about reconciliation. I am honored to participate in your book "Upon Arrival" In light of its reflection, I hope to inspire a writer to construct good poems. For me, this poem is one of the best I have written as it contains some pondering of myself, having it all, the best in life.*

## A Knock at My Door

Once upon a day in the past,
The devil came knocking on my door at last.
The person I was, at first turned away,
But his misery called my company and my decision began to sway.
I never saw the side he brought out in me,
she was risky and dangerous, something I never thought I could be.
Before I knew it he was with me everyday.
My brief hesitation grew to temptation, that wouldn't let me turn away.
The road we traveled, my brief buddy and me;
It was effortless, easy. . . inside I felt free,
I was blinded to the shackles and chains on my feet!
He presented them as a gift that was beautiful at the time,
But 2 years later I'm up at 5 am where from that destruction, birthed this rhyme.
It's funny how my life of success and self growth
Quickly fell from my hands, shattered, and on the floor it lay broke.
Time pays no mind to the gloomy or weak,
Time doesn't care if your standing still or moving your feet.
But as sure as the waves continuously greet the sands,
Time will move passed you or gladly hold your hand.
I can never undo what will forever be a part of my story,
I have to learn that life is what I make it, sadness or glory.
It's not how we stumble, it is not how we fall,
It is about how we rise up and continue standing tall.
Each and everyone us had to crawl, before we could walk the walk;
maybe this experience of weakness and shame will allow me to also talk the talk.
I know there's a light somewhere up ahead,
Just like after every storm the sun comes out again.
If the me I am now could only speak to the me that stood listening to that initial knock on my door,
I would tell her not to answer, keep those feet planted to the floor.

Lisa Colilla
*Keyport, NJ*

## Woman in the Moon

I see a face.
She is smiling.
She is speaking to me, but I can't make out the words.
I know your face.
And as I try to bring her into focus, the features change and is replaced by another.
I am like Scrooge.
My heart burns in truth and scorches me this night.
Faces that have forged their place in my mind, body and spirit.
I can never escape them, nor would I want to.
So beautiful.
It is she again.
Smiling, her beautiful free spirit within the moonlight and the shadowy crevasses of its surface.
What is thy purpose?
What are you trying to say?
Guide me sweet angel.
She is locked there too.
Unable to break her bonds and soar.
Fate is a stubborn dealing.
Something so fierce cannot be contained forever.
We will one day break these earthly irons sister and know blazing passion once more.

Kim Kowalski
*Middletown, CT*

## Here to Stay

I once was afraid but I am not anymore
In my crusade, my pen will open up the door
I'm ready for the rage. Bring on the tears
I will use this page to break through all my fears
I am a woman. I am strong
I am a woman. I belong
I have power, fire and innate desire
I am a woman. I am here to stay
Listen to me. We are more than just objects
Why can't you see? We are a force to be reckoned with
I am a woman. I am strong
I am a woman. I belong
I have power, fire and innate desire
I am a woman. I am here to stay
Put your will to the test
Don't stop until it's equal
Refuse to take less. In the end we are all people
I am a woman. I am strong
I am a woman. I belong
I have power, fire and innate desire
I am a woman. I am here to stay

Rachel Haines
*Montgomery, NY*

## Escapism

You'd end up mad with the life I've had
Giving away my flowers to whoever'd listen
I'm feeling faded like my jeans
My red eyes tear and glisten
With every hit I taste your lips
It sets off a cataclysmic explosion
It tightens up my lungs
I'm drowning in my own ocean
I've forgotten air's taste
I'm coughing up watery smoke
It doesn't matter how much I inhale
I'll never burn enough to choke
I'm addicted to escapism
I'm tired of simply hanging around
I want to feel free
I want my feet off the ground
I used to use sex, now I use drugs
Anything to feel less numb
There's a new light
And I see it when I flick my thumb

Kaitlyn Peelle
*Long Beach, CA*

*Hello, I'm a twenty-yaer-old college student on my way to becoming and English literature teacher. I've been battling mental illness for most of my life and poetry is my way of coping. Mental illness makes us feel alone in the world but that couldn't be less true. We're in this together. One love.*

## The Road I Took

I took a road
Around the bend
And off I strode
For time to spend
In my own head
To sit with my mind
In a moss filled bed
I happened to find
When I lost my way
And took a wrong turn
And wandered that day
When my heart did yearn
To find the answers I sought
Though I knew not the questions
I thought that I ought
Take nature's suggestions
So to a clearing I went
For there I was led
And hours I spent
In that moss covered bed
And though answers never came
The day, not forgotten
I shall come back just the same
To get more lost than I had gotten
To get lost in the unknown
Straight out of a book
With every stone
That's the road I took

Emily Reese
*Jamison, PA*

## Little Pill

With the help of a little magic pill.
All the problems in my life went away.
Fine, the pill may make me a little sick.
But take one a day and my head is all clear.
I can't remember not taking the pill.
I think that if I even tried to stop,
I've come too far to leave it in my past.
The pill is apart of me and my life.
Besides I don't want to quit my little pill.
It's my antidepressant after all.

Caitlin Macler
*Frisco, TX*

## Petty Tyrants

There are tyrants afoot in the land of the free
and the home of the brave.
They prey on those who are less than they.
Securing a sense of meaning from being
contemptuously demeaning,
Such lumbering lycanthropies, such tubs of guts.
These worthless popinjays with obscene struts.
Worshipping their egoistic tumescence as such
awe-inspiring excrescence,
When all they obtain is self-deluded domains;
such spewers of slop, such bloated stains

Fred Thomas Lee
*Vienna, WV*

## Crybaby Bridge

We all know a place near where we live
Of the nightmarish tale of Cry Baby bridge
A mother that threw her baby in the water
A horrible night that involved infant slaughter
In the middle of the bible belt outside a quaint farm town
That's where the real Cry Baby story unwound
It was a stormy night, water flooded field
The baby was crying and just would not yield
So mother bundled child and walked in a daze
To a bridge nearby where the water was raised
She stood on the bridge, said a prayer for the kid
And then she did what no parent has ever did
She tossed the crying baby into the drink
And with a smile on her face she watched the child sink
She walked away from the bridge and never seen again
The baby never recovered, Oh what a sin
Its said if you goto the bridge when the water flows just right
And you listen with your ears and close your eyes
You'll still hear the sound of when the little baby cries

Edward Hamilton
*Bloomingburg, OH*

*I have always been intrigued by folklore. The way that legends come to be and the lessons taught within have always interested me. The story of Crybaby Bridge is in about every state in the USA I find it remarkable how one story got adopted by so many other places. So the Crybaby Bridge poem was born. But my writings are always dedicated to my daughter Sydney Hamilton.*

## EUTHANASIA

With wisdom, who was more beloved than I?
Who grieves from emptiness, now so bereft
My knowledge fades to simple habits left
I can't maintain my memories, which fly
The dearest faces somewhere in the sky
Beclouded now, as by a gentle storm
That sprinkles raindrops on my blinded eyes
To change your face into a shapeless form
Propelling me toward unrelenting peace
That void where I shall be not cold nor warm
A lonely, bland and ever toneless norm
Where I am helpless to achieve release
  But you my love, beneath a fatal moon
  Decreed my final breath, too brief, too soon.

Maria Martinez
*Johnson City, NY*

*Maria Martinez, born in America, is a retired bridal seamstress and a grandmother of two. She likes to write poetry in English or Spanish but only as a hobby to share with family and friends. This sonnet was inspired by church teachings on the value of life.*

## The Best Part of My Heart

A lifetime of memories came rushing through his mind,
He did not want to leave.. but yet he knew that it was time,
Time to say goodbye... to move into the light,
The tunnel seemed so far away….. Yet it seemed so right.

He knew the end was near and it was time to go,
But before he left…….there was one thing she needed to know,
Although, they now would be so very far apart,
He wanted her to know "you have been the best part of my heart."

He laid there looking in her eyes with a smile on his face,
Dreaming of being pain free and in a better place,
Before he left he had to let her know how much he cared,
How happy he had been for the years that they shared.

He reached out and took her hand and held it very tight,
Wishing he could have….just one more day and one more night,
He realized his time was coming fast to an end,
She had been his wife and always his best friend.

If only somehow he could put all of this into words,
If only she would listen and believe just what she heard,
He spoke these final words and said, "While we will be far apart",
Remember always that you have been "the best part of my heart."

These few words have summed up a lifetime of love,
He now watches over her from heaven far above,
She looks into the stars at night and knows they are not so far apart,
Because he too was always "the best part of her heart."

Judith Slevin
*Nottingham, MD*

*My father died on October 6, 2005 from Lewy body's disease which is an aggressive form of Alzheimer's. ""My step-mother told me that before my dad died he looked into her eyes and told her "you are the best part of my heart."" I thought this was a beautiful way to sum up a life time together. My dad was a very sentimental and emotional man.*

## Treble/Trouble

You are a bunch of different versions of the same song.
And where she is perfect pictures all day at the park,
you are ugly sweaters and carving pumpkins at home.
You always heckled me to do better, about how I never smile
in pictures or brushed my teeth right after I ate breakfast.
You never could just sit there on the couch and watch a movie with me.
She's perfect you know?
She just wants what I want, she's the same song all the time.
She's consistent and she never gets drunk and cries over silly
things like the way my favorite shirt never quite balances
on the hanger correctly.
She's not you.
She doesn't sit at the piano silently and wait for the sun
to hit the middle G key at exactly 9am.
She likes to cook.
You are high heels for no reason, and curly hair all over my face.
Where she is skinny, in converse and with perfect make up,
you are big and stand tall and will not take no for an answer.
You were my first love, but not my last.
I am not sorry that I let you leave.
If you love something you let it go right?
I just hope you never come back.
Where I am strong and flexible,
You have always made me weak and stubborn.
If you were to come home, I pray to never see you. I pray that
you never find me and her sitting at her favorite sushi
restaurant, the one that you would pass by every day because
you liked the plastic sushi replicas in the window.

Anastasia Quinn
*Charlottesville, VA*

## Atlas Drowns

Yesterday I saw Atlas drown
Grasping at me with desperate hands,
He wants nothing more than to pull me down
His strangled cries a dark command
Those depths sing siren wails of awful times
Heartbeat rabbit-quick, staccato drums in humming dark
But I find no calm in his tempest
I find no solace in his bleeding heart
He finds any weight he can hold,
Back broken with the strain of his own burden
And as I pluck myself from his shoulders,
He sinks into the ocean
I thought myself one to stab Atlas
To drive my knife into his thighs
I dreamt to watch him fall
While I placed the stones that let him rise
Because doesn't Atlas know?
It's his burden that lets him fly
Wouldn't Atlas stop to think?
He holds not the world, but the sky

Leah Colligan
*Howard, GA*

## Unknown Scars

Fields are now cities
Trees are now homes
The world we see
Is more than we've roamed
The hills and the valleys
Were once still alive
And the history of them
Was forced to die
The pain and the loss
Of our trusting friend
Was stabbed in the back
With our own dirty hands
Why can't we just cherish
The moments we have
Instead we must fight
On this innocent land
If the trees could talk
If the dirt could speak
The stories they have
Would make us weak
They witness murder
They witness pain
They know what happened
Yet they grow our grain
They save our lives
Every dreadful day
And the harsh things we do
Will never go away.

Shelby Owens
*Logandale, NV*

## Sacrifice

No one ever talks about the sacrifice
No one ever tells you that once you've given yourself to someone there may be nothing left for you
He told me I was beautiful
The rich mosaic that comprised my soul
No one told him how mosaics are made
Piece by broken piece that I alone have managed to replace
That years of trauma chipped away at my very being
Making those mosaic tiles
No one told him that my soul was once a whole being
That life had slowly broken down piece by piece
I plastered back together the remnants I could find
No one ever tells you that even demons put to sleep will one day rise
Tucking them to bed one day the mask could someday fall
The ether dripped upon that mask the well could someday dry
Instead of handing plaster he decided not to replace the tiles as they fell
Until there was nothing left of ME at all
Swept away the pieces, ripped apart my soul
It's up to me now
To search and find the tiles.
To search and find the masks
To pacify my demons, and rectify my life

Sharona Campbell
*Austin, AR*

## Heart Wrenching

I hope in a different life you chose me
Because if this life is all we have
It'd be a catastrophe
I hope in the next life
Things turn out differently
Sometimes we feel like a Shakespeare play
How everyone dies by the end
The story that's predictable
A love story turned tragedy
I hope in a different life you chose me
Because if this is all we have
How heart wrenching it would be

Cynthia Snyder
*Endwell, NY*

## Legna, the Little Angel

Legna never understood how she got her name, it sounded very different than other children's names. She asked her mother why she ever named her this and her mother told her she named her with a "twist." Oh my, said Legna, with a twist, is that how I became to exist? When you were born, I wanted a name different from those who had the same. You are so special and so dear you must have a name to celebrate from year to year. So if you look at your name and turn it backwards it reads the same—my little Legna -Angel!

Deborah Wilcoxson
*Venice, FL*

## Medusa

Go ahead, scream your battle cry,
And ignore my tears,
I look up at you through a foggy haze from where I lay,
How is it that your face seems to possess no fears?
It holds valor, glory, accomplishment…
And a smile…
How can you smile with such ease?
What did you even accomplish?
My further torturement?
Whoo-hoo for you.
At this point,
I'd beg you to kill me, I'd even add in a please…
But alas… that would require you to listen
And my current curse to be lifted…
Yes, I called it a curse;
My existence, my life, my horrid power…
But to see one smile with such glee,
I can't bare to plea,
For it would alert you of your failure.
Even when your goal is my end,
I can't bare to see another face falter
All because of me and my strong resilience to the end.

Lauren MacLean
*Brighton, MI*

## Not a Label

You are not a label.
Your thoughts are not simply for sale.
Your height and weight and gender
are not what makes you you.
You are not your age, nor
previously lived place.
Your identity is not determined
solely by your face.
What really makes you are your favorite tunes.
Lyrics that stick in your head, and your thoughts from
morning 'til bed.
You are the person
you choose to be,
from your favorite books to what you watch on TV.
You are beautiful and profound.
You're when your head's in the clouds
but your feet are on the ground.
You are a thousand things, but people only seem to see
the million things you simply cannot be.
They'll try to hurt you, to tell you
you're not enough.
But no matter their taunts,
know it's a fable,
because you are simply
not a label.

Amara Barney
*Suisun, CA*

*Hey there! I'm fifteen years old and a member of the Church of Jesus Christ of Latter Day Saints. I enjoy playing the piano, drawing, painting, writing, speaking French, and being goofy with all my wonderful friends. I also enjoy singing but I'm horrible at it so . . . Yeah. Anyways, take this poem how you will, but I believe being you no matter the circumstances because every single person is beautiful and the world needs to see that. So be you and be free.*

## Ghost

I've seen your face a million times, yet I haven't seen you in what feels like a million years.
I've forgotten your features, the curve of your smile, and the furrow of your brows.
I long to touch you and be touched by you.
I want to disappear, disappear inside your heart, to sink into your soul, to bond to your bones.
I miss your face.
I haven't seen you in a million years.
You've become a vision to me.
You've become a long lost treasure, a treasure that remains lost, a wonder of the world.
I've seen your face a million times, but I'm embarrassed to say I don't know what you look like.
I miss you.
My thoughts of you are so ethereal, yet so impure.
You haunt me and betwixt me.
You've become my ghost.
My romantic faceless dream fading in and out.
I light candles, read scripture, and keep our memories to come, alive.

Charmaine Gills
*Oklahoma City, OK*

## Black-Hearted Eve

For sins committed she's forever bound
to endless flight the earth around.
Floating aloft on a long black veil.
With evening comes her mournful wail.
She wears an ancient face and long black hair.
Beneath her veil fogs cold night air.
From the warm of day to the shiver of night
Eve of morrow chases the light.
Flowers in the garden hide their heads in fear
of the cold black eyes in the face drawing near.
Her long dark shadow follows the end of day.
Still no remorse for her evil way.
No one knows how foul her deed
or why she can never be freed.
But there is one thing we know for sure
her heart is far from being pure.

Leroy Cole
*Indianapolis, IN*

*After four years with the army security agency, I worked for the US Navy in the field of naval weapon systems until retirement. I live in Indianapolis, IN, with my wife Rose. My hobbies include restoring antiques, writing, and art. I practice rhyming words and have notebooks full of them. Poems come from imagination and inspiration from past experiences and daily life.*

## I Am Here

In a world of deprivation
There's a need for revitalization
Intuition runs wild
Capture each moment in Mother Earth eyes
Leave the lurking beast where he hides
Trust that no one else can ensemble pride
Believe that dreams fulfill inside
Bursting with laughter calm the inner child
Love that goes beyond reason
Devouring each moment in each season
Lust for the deed that hasn't been done yet
The signature in the stone has been set
No guarantees in life as of yet
Familiarity for death takes innocent breath
Consciously invoking spirits of regret
Unravel the world that thirst for richness
Today will be the day...we continue to say
Devour the non gluten of life's fairy-tale days
Overhung by mandated reparation
Who else could live like this each day
Goodbye fear, Goodnight tears, so long wasted years
Shout to the world *I am here!*

Traibiyah Brown
*Cleveland, OH*

## I Witnessed Her Depart with the Coming Tide

I witnessed her depart with the coming tide
Her eyes were closed and her lips moved in silence
The grandeur of her soul felt a rush
The purity of her heart a shush
She looked right through me with a smile
I felt as though I had known her a small while
And overcome by the festering burn of loss
Her hand being the only warmth I sought
She looked forward and walked toward the sand
I as the child blown by the wind
Bent by the stronger will
The lenient sorrow of tomorrow
The numb moment that comes from a skiff
Beckoned by the shadow of inner want
Her hand slowly slipped from mine
Upon my palm I feel it still
Her light footsteps crossed the land and water line
Her clothes billowed around
The feet which never touched the ocean's ground
A wave appeared as I had feared
The last I saw of her were eyes
Full of love and remorseful goodbyes
Time is but a substance none can lend
We promised we would be until the end
None can say she once ever lied
I witnessed her depart with the coming tide

Jurnee Acosta
*Lancaster, PA*

## Cuts

Being hurt by a friend is like getting a cut.
It hurt for a little bit but, heals and sometimes even goes away.
And then life eventually goes back to normal.
Being hurt by family is like getting cut,
and it leaves a scar.
It may feel, and the pain may go away.
But the scar will also be there to remind you,
of the ones that hurt you the most.

Mike Bunn Jr.
*Muscatine, IA*

## August 14th

I fought bears to reach the peak.
My worst enemy, conquered.
At peace within, I've killed the ego and faced the shadows.
Serene and Whole.
Symbolic, Spiritual & Infinite.
Rightfully so, the views and gifts fit for all the kings and queens.
Among the peaks, hawks own their flight.
Gliding in their freedom.
Emotional baggage dropped, eloquently drifted,
Reminiscing on those shooting stars, the final night.
I have forgiven myself, so let's sit in our power;
Vast, Just, Beautiful & Thankful.

Christian Castaneda
*Boulder, CO*

**Dear High School Graduates:**

The world is scary
The fears, the anxiety, the stress
They tell us it changes as we get older
but with age comes responsibility
We are the ones responsible for our futures
not the ones who held our hands
The clock keeps ticking
No longer are we carefree
We are an age of worry, but
We are also an age of hope
We demand change in ourselves, yet
We are hopeful for a new experience
Hope for safety and for security
We wrap ourselves in pictures
to say who we want to be
To give a facade of who we can be
if we tried
The world is full of terrible people, and
we are told
As the clock keeps ticking,
We become older
We become wiser
We become anxious
We are hopeful
(Now read from the bottom to the top)

Victoria Vermillion
*Commack, NY*

## The Fire Was Never Understood

I am happy that you know me.
That you know my actual name.
For I am not the parent of the devil.
That you have dipped your hands inside me.
And I'm not what they say I am.
My rage is deadly—yes, I understand.
But so is water, earth and the sky when stirred with anger.
You say that water has drowned you further than the marks
left by my red, orange and yellow.
Those marks you fear not, for they will heal.
They will become stones of red.
And leave you with new skin.
Mix me with sand and I'll become magic of warm blanket on your body.
For all the sand must be bathing with the ever persistent blue.
I promise you that the deep sea will devour you with its many
monsters harboring inside.
I for once will become your sun—making sure you never sleep next to
my death.
And if you ever wear red, orange or yellow, you'll blend in with me.
For water will wash them off.
And worse—it will refuse to blend, leaving you transparent, alone.
Once you wear red, orange or yellow, we'll twirl in twists and turns.
Together, no one will notice who's burning.
For the ones who burn terrify of burning.
And for the ones who light only stay longer to keep alive—at least until
the sun snores far away.
The moon might keep the sky some company.
How selfish it is—it's forgotten you.
Its hopeless love to the sky never concerns you to the moon.
And I—your selfless lover—I stay inside for your tall walls.

Hinaa Noor
*Bayonne, NJ*

## Comet

Black and white steer
The furry first-born of the herd
Perfect, but trapped
Caged within the walls of pneumonia

He tried and tried
Weeks after the diagnosis;
Weeks after countless shots,
And Mom telling me he might not make it
And already shushing my silent, hopeful tears

We sat at the Greene County Fair, glad he made it
Hoping his heavy breathing wouldn't return
But soon we saw his rough, pink tongue
Gasping for air.

Each time we went into the ring
With me on the end of our the halter
His breathing went normal
And the next thing I know the judge
Is shaking my hand
And handing me the second place ribbon
Now all the cattle people
Are asking me questions
And Comet's licking his prize
Finally feeling all right

Molly Mossing
*Cedarville, OH*

## The Man, the Addiction

He looks her over—up and down—slowly,
He gently touches her, looking for imperfections.
He makes a deal and rubs her side,
"Don't worry, baby, we're going to take good care of you."
He takes her home, undresses her layer by layer,
looking for bumps, bruises, and wrinkles.
The process starts, layers of primer,
layers of foundation, more layers of foundation,
the wrinkles and blemishes finally covered.
Then the layers of blush,
fine strokes that redefine the lines.
Finally, she is done.
Dressed in layers of ghost lines
Standing—waiting for her name to be called,
as if she were an anxious girl at her first cotillion.
He is nervous, waiting for her to ascend.
Finally, it's her turn,
the metal shade goes up and the spider web gate opens;
she slowly floats down the ramp to the oohs of the crowd.
He smiles and nods his head.
The crowd looks her over. She's SOLD!
Her chrome shines brightly as if she is proud to be there,
He kisses her gently, silent tears run down his face,
"Always, remember you are one of mine."
"Drive FAST! Drive HARD! Drive LOUD! Make me PROUD!"

Tammy Johnson
*Sergeant Bluff, IA*

*I am very lucky to do what I love—writing, teaching, and spending time with my family. My husband Carl of forty years is my biggest supporter. The inspiration for this poem is Danny, aka "Count" Koker from Counting Cars. My husband and I love the show. We were watching one night and saw how Danny talked to the cars, looked them over, and even in the finished process talks to the cars and sometimes he cries silent tears when he lets them go.*

## Safe

Silently drifting through
the water
as the moon lights up
the sky
I can see the horizon
my rescue the boat sailing by
In the darkness of the
water
I hear the crashing of
the waves
wishing for an answer
please don't go away
rescue me
can you please save me
from this place
I've never been
safe within

Yvette Bukoffsky
*Beaufort, SC*

## I Try

I try very hard,
You must believe me.
I try to be positive.
I try to get good grades.
I try to socialize.
I try not to cry.
I try to smile.
I try to laugh.
I try to be nice.
I try to be happy.
I do all the things I'm suppose to do.
Why isn't it working for me.
I wipe my tears,
Force my laugh,
Fake my smile,
And pretend that I'm okay.
Just like any other day.

Magen Darling
*Hannibal, NY*

## The Bathtub

Someone left the bathtub filled up again.
Clawed feet, copper faucet, a plug at the end of a silver chain.
No one pulled that plug.
The space between a drain and a drain with purpose is someone else's choice.
No one ever promised this would be fair.
Someone sticks their arm into the cold water.
"I'm taking matters into my own hands."
Another someone cuts that arm off.
No one ever promised this wouldn't be fraught.
A red sea, a floating limb.
"That's going to stain."
Porcelain
suggestible
impressionable.
The one-armed someone leaves and comes back with a bucket.
"You can't get rid of me that easy."
Another someone stabs a hole in that bucket.
No one ever promised effort would be respected.
"You're making a mess. Sit down."
Eventually, the bathroom gets crowded.
No one cares about what the tub wants.
No one has even asked.

Jenna Ribbing
*West Hollywood, CA*

## Self-Conscious

I am under the stare of the whole world
Even when no one is looking at me.
Pressure from my own thoughts can keep me up
Or lull me to sleep.
Moments where I believe in validation crumble
Under the song of doubt;
Always playing and wreaking havoc.
Am I alone?
Looking into the crystal surface of torment
I am reminded of my sins.
How much good can appear in life
Before it must be evened out by bad?
If I count things in odds I will be punished
If I count in evens I can live for another day.
Everything in moderation...How?
Am I alone? Physiologically, I'm alone.
Physically, I surrounded by support.
It is my own journey
Yet I share the thoughts of many.

Chloe Thorburn
*Robinson, TX*

## Love Restores

The way coffee
stimulates your brain,
love restores
the tired parts of your soul.

Sheldon Hubbard
*Argos, IN*

*I was sitting at work one morning, sipping my velvety black Folgers when the first line of the poem came to me. Throughout the day, I pushed the rest of it out and wrote it in my phone notes. It reminds me that no matter how bogged down by life's happenings you may be, love will always restore what has been so ravaged,especially honesty and unconditional love—something I have the pleasure of sharing with my wife, our dogs, and our community. When you put love first, everything else makes a little more sense in the end. God bless.*

## Bury Me Alive

Bury me alive inside the inner chambers of your heart
So if you ever need me, you'll know I'm never far
If the world comes crashing down, you'll never be alone
But if you need a reason to live...
Baby, you're better off on your own
I counted the pieces of us-
As you started to break
What we had became broken—
Then you slipped away
The light in your eyes grew dark
What happened to you?
We're less than lovers now
You've become a stranger too

Kristen Brown
*Calhoun City, MS*

## Engaging Humanity

Everyone on every continent is affected by what's going on today
Trade wars, market fluctuations, political debacles and more...
Space junk falling, shootings, global warming, drought, famine
Unknown results to these issues is what is for sure

Heads of government or political party
No one person should control life, death and/or the destiny...
Of displaced persons, migrants, refugees, immigrants
Because we do not know what the future will bring to you or me

Know that we are all brothers and sisters, every man and woman
Regardless of race, color, creed, orientation or national origin...
Hope, love and joy are sought by us all, every minute, every day
If we can all live in harmony, then and only then peace can begin

For today's world we cannot expect the past norms in life
As we are living in ever changing dubious times today...
There is no norm or status quo that can be upheld - seek change
Look around, do your best to be part of that change, I'd say

In seeking change, expect for there to be challenges
Be mindful of right and wrong, good and bad...
What is wrong may not be so bad and
What is right may not always be good, so sad
Engaging humanity to live in harmony for the rest of their life
Seek happiness for old, young, Mom, Dad, child, husband, wife!

Saundra Russell
*Tucson, AZ*

## Addiction

My "everything in moderation" is broken
My off switch doesn't work
It twists and turns
It pulls me in
Leaves me fighting just for air
It's food, it's drugs, it's sex, it's drinks
Every single time I think I've got this
It can't control me
There it is to reach out and hold me down
That vice
Its got me
Its sitting on top of me
I might go a day, a month, or a year
How did I even wind up here?
The food, the drugs, the sex, the drinks
Makes it so I cant even think
And all it does is hold me down
It always starts with a sweeping declaration
I'll never do that to myself again
Which usually I've broken before the days end
Self-loathing creeps in
It envelops my skin
The food, the drugs, the sex, the drinks
Makes it so I cant even think clearly
And all it does is hold me down
How do I explain that it came before you
The cycle of addiction
That pierces me through and through
It drags me, it pulls me, it sits just below me
The food, the drugs, the sex, the drinks
Makes it so I can't even think

Megan Lightner
*Calhan, CO*

## Eighteen Seasons

Eighteen seasons came and went
Where your youth was spent,
On bruised elbows and skinned knees
From climbing all those tall trees.
Mud was your favorite way to dress,
Though, not your Sunday best.
Your youthful ways have now been said and done,
Oh! such a beautiful one!
I thank God everyday that your were the little child
Loaned to me,
And sad though it may be,
It is time to set you free.
Upon the world to contribute your talents and dreams,
Yes, even some hair-brained schemes.
To make a new life away from me.
Although, I will always be able to see
You turn around and smile that little boy grin,
I won't ever show my heart breaking within.

Gloria Thoma Miller
*Butler, PA*

## What Is a Fiction Writer?

A mindful multitasker making multitudinous mysteries,
with the mix of mitigating most miscellaneous miseries.
They're a retaliating rebel
resuscitating relics for revival,
refusing redundant replications
recollected in recitals.
Picture a predecessor predating paleolithic passages,
proving parallel polarities
possible through passiveness.

I'm a neoteric nomad navigating through neon nebulas,
nimble on a nimbus, not so normal, never was;
or a kid collectively connecting kinetic calligraphy,
because kaleidoscopes can characterize continually.
Although my dialect can mimic derelicts,
this diagram demonstrates
dialogue past demigods destined to delineate.

Truly, we're transcendentalists
training to try out telepathy,
time traveling through teleportation telekinetically.
Put simply,
we're supernovas, signaling series of synonyms,
as if we're synecdoches for
serializing sociocentric syndicates!

Josiah Gingras
*North Oxford, MA*

## Breaking the Chains

Stuck in a prison with my hands attached to a wall.
No escape from the cold steel on my aching wrists.
Locked in the dark jail cell with people like me.
A place that others put me in without my say.
My mind stuck in a loop, wondering what life could be.
The writing utensil within my hand,
tallying the days until I can be free.
All that I do must be in secret, or they will hear.
And if they hear, they move me to a different cell.
They will take me away from the friends I just made.
And strip me of all my joy.
As the days go by, it just gets harder and harder.
But looking out the window always reminds me that,
one day I'll be released from my mental hell.
The day that I'll be "Breaking the Chains."

Jack Dunlap
*Cresco, PA*

**If a Tree Acts in a Forest...**

If all the world's a stage, I am tree five.
Rooted back where "actors" "act" to feel "alive,"
Romeo tells an old forlorn aside,
The gallery loves the tale, I deride.
Look, see the tree behind the lover's hue?
With plastic limbs and cardboard cover too.
Could he, the scorned fifth tree, play many parts?
Well certainly not, in the rear of art.
Would galleries gasp if I blurred stage lines?
To front the lover, I find asinine.
This tree may have his own tall tale to tell,
And this script dwells in hell. Would mine as well?
They'll never know the story I'd derive;
For all the world's a stage, and I, tree five.

Joseph Penrod
*Sioux Falls, SD*

## Vineyard of Endless Love

What is love?
Having given all out
as said: love is all fair and yet war
Love is kind and love is giving.
No other truer fight to give greatest than those hearts that we hold such love for, to ease our own suffering and selfish needs to conquer the demons of our own hearts to be complete and whole once more enter restore order to fade away the dark that only one's heart to another can repair by even a flicker of light held.
Even held by the very touch and our darkest path to warm the very wounds and cut by flesh with shed blood and the same fight of giving yet a heart of such means even if broken and shattered laying like glass and a million pieces has the same power of only known cure for pain is beauty As It seeps like wine deep within our own veins working hard hearts like chasing after midnight kisses and nights dreams by staying up on Ecstasy of flooded teardrops bottled up of the thoughts adrift at sea. we give and take letting it take over us!, breaking our bones in the process of the very act to fight in pulsating hearts very wine takes over that breath we try to catch watching our bones turn to dust fading in a cloud forming in the sun lit sky of another day to make memories and chase after another's heart to be held .

Stacey Johnson
*Gallatin, TN*

## Ballet Girl

tall and broad, fair and strong, light and dusk
The dichotomy of us
soft in touch, gleaming love, untamed heart
undiscovered work of art

you take the seeing route on this ground
and triumph in the solace here and now
but there's a piece of you that can't be found
a soft, pink toe pointing down

you knew your dreams far too late
I pray you'll be that ballet girl someday
you missed your chance, said no to the bird
there is beauty in the topside of the world

standing firm and concerned tuning hymns
another life begins
outstretched hands, understand, love and woos
your dreams can be made new

You see Him now plie away
I prayed for that ballet girl to save
you reach the stars and start to twirl
there is beauty in the topside of the world

Rachael Ballish
*Athens, OH*

## Death Road

Scraps of metal laying upon the rough road
They say she didn't make it
It becomes increasingly hard to breath
My mind spins in a hundred directions
As I sit along the road sobbing
I ask why
Why must he take her
For she did nothing wrong
They say she had no chance
A self implode on contact
I yell I scream I kick I stomp
Yet nothing changes
Hasn't my family been through enough
I feel as if depressed
This feeling comes and goes
For her smile her touch her voice her laugh
All got ripped away
My heart is now all but empty
To myself I think
Maybe I'll see her one day

Jordyn Tynsky
*Decatur, TX*

## Risk

I have a dream, I want to live;
Being adventurous, taking a chance, desiring us.
Finding meaning to those unspoken words,
Risking my soul to your love.
They call me intuitive,
Fighting the world, attaining my dreams.
What if, this time I lose;
And, you continue to be my dream.

Pooja Banerjee
*New York, NY*

## Angels

Angels full of love sent to us from God above to say our prayers in God's light we are shielded from our fight. To protect Americans dreams from all our obscenities and blasphemy when we're out of touch our subconscious minds takes a shadow of our first mental state of minds when we go to pitch real far a home run not very far.

Bridgette Ballard
*Apache Jct, AZ*

*As I evolve as an individual I hope to prosper from the knowledge I receive to better the quality of my life's work. I see the reader bettering the quality of their life as they read my work. I hope you prosper as you acquire the knowledge of others. I thank you for your time to get to know me for my work. Knowledge is the only way we can better the quality of our life and the people who know us and for those who can relate to our writing, God bless you.*

## Once, I Was a Child

Once, I was a child, and I would jump in the puddles,
In my yellow rain boots.
Once, I was a child, and I asked trick or treat.
To the unsuspecting neighbor who lived on my block.
Once, I was a child, and I scraped my first knee.
My mother patched it up and kissed it with love.
Once, I was a child, and I made my first friend.
Sharing secrets and making promises.
Once, I was a child, and I had my first snowfall.
Making snowmen outback with hot cocoa inside.
Once, I was a child, and I rode my first bike.
As dad held me up and I pedaled my feet.
Once, I was a child, and I played in the ocean.
The waves on my face and the salt in my hair.
Once, I was a child, and I saw my first sunset.
The bright colors saying good night.
I'm no longer a child, but I still jump in puddles.
In my yellow rain boots.

Margot Englander
*Philadelphia, PA*

## Mystic Lands

White unicorns and black pegasus's;
Red, green dragon's flying overhead;
Pixies and fairies playing amongst the flowers;
Cotton candied mountaintops.
Golden Hawks and silver bears;
Gargoyles circling, protecting;
Chestier cats prancing for hours;
Red and black licorice fields.
Grey wolves and white ponies;
Black cerebus's walking, vigilant;
Albino squirrels eating from my hand;
White chocolate raindrops.
Orange owls and pink, blue tigers;
Harpies leaping about, guarding;
The Cyclops to play a friendly game with;
Cherry slushy streams.
Mystic lands, my troubles escape;
Far away, nothing can get me here;
Safe inside, from the horrors outside;
My personal secure surreal vision.

Ron Vernon
*Plattsmouth, NE*

## Wishes, Merely

What is the bond that binds us as one?
Is it a red string among our pinkies?
Or the wishes we blow through a dandelion?
Is it merely hope; to hold someone and to be held?
I ask myself this, often pondering on the possibilities.
I think to myself, getting lost in my thoughts.
People ask me what I believe and think,
I merely tell them 'nothing worth while'
Of which its true, but they still worry.
I met a man from my past, I had wronged him.
He was quick to forgive.
I wondered why he did this.
Why does he care?
How can a man so kind, be around me?
The man had been around for some time,
Our bond grew more, we are bound by a red string.
Or so we thought, I worried for I couldn't see it.
Was it truly there? Or were we just united by the wishes;
The wishes that travel through a dandelion.
They can be strong in our hearts, but not truly.
No matter how strong they seem, they can still break.
When they break, we break too.

Gavin Mitchell
*Johnson City, TN*

## The Brown Americans—A Poem of Liberty and Justice

We lay down your highways and sewer lines
We build your homes and bridges
In all sorts of inclement weather
We mine your ores and ship your freight
We clean your bathrooms and cook your meals
We teach your small children the mysteries of life
And give them laughter and joy
Our soldiers fight honorably in our American wars
And die upon foreign battlefields with you
We shed our blood for the freedom of all
We mourn our losses with tears of grief
And our tears fall upon the American nation
Where we bury our dead next to yours
Yet, we are the Hispanic Americans
Not invited to sit with you at the table of justice
We are lessors and discounted
in the participation of the democratic process
We suffer the pain of rejection
You say we are not a distinct race
But only a "cultural heritage"
Who are not qualified to receive civil rights protections
Or those privileges granted other racial minorities
We are brown – but you say we are Caucasians
Yet you do not treat us as Caucasians
We are La Raza Unita
and we seek only equal recognition and respect
Though we are the brown Americans –
We are Americans just the same as you
Who share in the same vision for this great land
Of which we embrace as our homeland too

Samuel Allen
*Denver, CO*

## Practicing for Heaven

Most of the music I've written will never see the light of day
I guess it wasn't meant to be heard here
But that's okay because still I persevere
Driven by a sense that it's not for nothing

That there's an eternity coming…

Where the symphonies in my head will finally be scored
Where the walls will play back their tapes
Where all of the ideas, those remembered and those long forgotten,
will proclaim that it's time

Where all the years of practice will reveal that it has been for
something;
that I was being honed for the ultimate performance

Or maybe not…

Maybe it was just for the sheer pleasure of it
To be enjoyed only within the confines of the finite
And that's okay too
But I really don't believe that…

Andrew Baffi
*Clinton Corners, NY*

## One Woman's Story About Perseverance

Have you ever taken the time to ask yourself,
What is it that is inside of you that drives you, in making you want to succeed?
My answer is Perseverance.
I come from a broken home
where the word family is foregin to me
and the word survival is comforting.
You see I never wanted to be unbreakable,
but my whole life I spent being broken.
I never wanted to be forced to work it out,
but my whole life I had to make it work.
I give myself a pep talk,
telling myself it is time to stop contracting excuses
But to trust the fact that beauty will be the outcome of my struggle,
There is no other time than now,
to start raising my truth.
I am grateful for choice
and
what perseverance has got me through

Jessica Charest
*Worcester, MA*

## Burnt Ends

I was a
firecracker.
Vibrant, loud and bursting
with light.
But when I lost you, every
light in my world
went dark.
Now I am only
burnt ends. Charred and
alone.

Rebecca DiFede
*Morris Plains, NJ*

## A Day Before Us

Before I reached you, not so far yet not so close.
Before I saw you, the first step to noticing others.
Before the night you took off the mask,
hiding your true feelings.
Before getting close, a knot that gives assurance.
Before our lips touched, the starting point of all changes.
Before you and I became we, the final destination
of friendship to lovers.
Before confessing love,
There was a day before us!

Jake Casella
*Northford, CT*

## Agustin Ramos López—Our Dad, Our Greatest Treasure

There is *no* amount of gold
That this world can measure
Agustin Ramos López

Our dad—our greatest treasure

Humbleness and honesty
You bestow on us each day
Through your acts of kindness
Your serenity incandescence our way

Six hearts beat from our mother and your divinity
Given as remembrance from God above
Each one of your children is precious
Filled with faith, hope and love

Augustine is your courage and mind
Daniel is your character and conviction
Jesus is your champion and warrior
Gerardo, alongside his wife, Virginia,
Is your legacy through their son Noah Andres
Teresa is your adoration for she is your only daughter,
Nurturing her children
Juan Agustin, Silvina Elaine and Carli Teresa
Rumaldo is the embodiment of your soul and strength

We all hold in our eyes
An image of our mother, your wife.
The mirror that breathes God,
We are love and we are full of life.

Words cannot express the gift of you
There is no greater endeavor
*Agustin Ramos López*
Our dad
Our greatest treasure

Daniel López
*Bellaire, TX*

## And One Day

And one day, your time will come.
Hopefully not as early as some.
You will close your eyes and be at peace-
No more sorrow, no more weeps.
Death will arrive at its own pace,
For life is a marathon, not a race.
Enjoy every moment!
Every chapter of the book,
And have no regrets when you take a final look,
And one day, your time will come.
It shall not be painful.
There will be no strife,
For you will have enjoyed your life.
The scraped knees, the broken hearts,
The bumpy roads and the lessons learned,
All the times the tables turned.
One day, you'll be ready.
You'll be content.
Nothing like you've ever dreamt-
And that day, your time will come.

Ellie McClellan
*Charlotte, NC*

*I am seventeen years old and live in a family of five. My mom, dad, and brothers have always supported me. From the age of thirteen, I lived away from home to train for figure skating. Competitive skating has taught me countless life lessons and the meaning of hard work. Poetry has always been a way for me to escape and cope with stress and depression. This specific poem is about learning how to enjoy life and not dwell on the idea of death. We can't let the fear of death control our lives.*

## My Love

When we first met, I was floored by your magnificent manners and charismatic charm.
My heart flicked and fluttered, my palms sappy and sweated, and face flushed and warm.
I did tell you quickly quiet down while the prominent pastor belted out his sermon and song.
You broke through my brutish barriers that I held onto for so long.
We've both been through the chill of ice and heated deserts of time.
But still we hold steadfastly strong. I am yours...you are mine.
God gregariously, beautifully blessed us by having us meet.
What an awesome and amazing feat!
I am forever totally thankful for that day and this.
I am so lucky and in laughter and love with you...never knew there could be so much bounty and bliss.
I know I haven't been prim and perfect, but I know I lusciously love you so.
I love you so much my loving love, I hope all hope…I know you know.
You are so ingeniously intelligent, thoughtful, giving, and kind.
You seriously send me to another playful plane…a marvelous and merry state of mind.
I think the world of you...if you ever go... I will miserably miss.
I say this to you my love, love, my love...I will seal this with a caressing kiss.

Sonia Langiano
*Sevierville, TN*

## Resilience

I woke up today to see
a quite whole different me,
a girl who is making better choices
someone who is living free.
In a world with no more pain
workin' like I've got something to gain.
Today I'm feeling just a little bit lucky,
family and friends no longer trying to "duck me."
I want to do right
each new day and every night.
I'm waking up early
and I'm seeing the light
the past is the past
and I gave up the fight.
I'm going to walk down my street
and greet each person I meet
with my chin in the air
no looking down, nothin' to see there.
I've picked myself up before
and I'll do it again
'cause my life-once a struggle
I thought I'd never win.
So, now it's time to define
the whole "new" me- priorities re-arranged
to show the world how great I can be.

Angela Fulk
*Howell, MI*

## The Sum of One's Parts

Is it easier? To imagine one's object of desire
As simply the sum of its parts, atomized
Cores of nuclei within clouds of electrons;
Or the concept of love, as serotonin and oxytocin,
Chemicals, cold and absolute.
Why is it that dissection can reduce something as
Beautiful as you are to something elementary,
Something not worthy of loving?
Perhaps we are afraid, not of each other, but of our
Capacity to feel;
Our emotions so intense that we overflow,
Their weight leaking through our eyes, our mouths.
We are scared of ourselves,
So we scrutinize, and we probe, and we beat to death
Those we love; turn them into butterflies,
Preserved carefully and pinned down on a corkboard,
As beautiful as they were the day they
Crawled out of their cocoons,
But dead and stinking of formaldehyde.

Valerie Fu
*Sunnyvale, CA*

## Child's Play

Still, serene, cosmic scene,
Dancing in the twilight 'fore dusk.
Gentle summer breeze, floors of green,
In God's creation I trust.
Away from the streets, the busy speed,
The needs, the deeds, and the fees.
As the trees recite their creed, come, follow me,
Away from the bustle and flux.
And then I lend my ear to hear what this creator is telling me.
The flurry of gust drops in,
Up, down, left and right,
Not in disarray, but rehearsed untroubled maneuvers,
As if He breathed, and waved through the countless timber fingers.
As if in that moment, the gust,
Gave them life, made them youthful,
Dancing in the breeze, simple,
Child's play.
And I notice the daffodil, right by my feet,
And recall what Sir William had said,
Daffodil on its own, had anyone known
Seen it unique, apart from the rest?
And then did I see,
What was being said to me
A unity, purpose at best.
Cause how could the tree be without the leaves,
Each purpose, large or small, must commence.

Nathan Trznadel
*Virginia Beach, VA*

## The Angered Tree

The howling winds pierced my stone heart
I was a statue above your still corpse
My eyes frozen in place
Fixated deeply on the soaked tree
And the massive branch it had thrown
At my distracted soul
But in a split second
Your bravery and selflessness
Angered the menacing tree
Who hurled the monstrous branch
Onto your innocent body
Looming over us
Casting a sinister shadow
That engulfed my soul
The looming tree was violently shaking
By the powerful winds of the raging storm
As if it were trying to mock me
For being a coward

Devika Amalkar
*Allen, TX*

*I am a sophomore in high school. I would describe myself as an artistic person as I have been learning dance and piano for many years and have enjoyed drawing, painting, and writing as hobbies. I feel that all of these art forms are beautiful ways to express emotions and feeling. I have always had an interest in poetry since I was in kindergarten and would often write poems for my mom to stick on the fridge. I wanted "The Angered Tree" to convey the narrator's guilt through metaphor and personification as well as create a dark and sinister tone.*

## Intoxicated

You can find me sober, I couldn't get drunk enough off
of you.
Like the squeeze of lime, you licked the salt off my
rim, and left a bitter taste on my lips.
I never did like the taste of whiskey.
Now it's a reminder, maybe I never liked you.
I was fixated on a list of ingredients for a drink
that didn't exist.
Maybe, it was just me trying to pour tequila
over your gin.
And if I mixed long enough I would feel
what you feel, but I don't.
Maybe we can still talk, maybe we'll remain
friends.
But, I can't keep drowning myself in feelings,
I don't feel.
Even if I once did.
I am no longer intoxicated, I am thinking
a lot clearer now.
You had your chance, the bar is now closed.

Stephanie Moreno
*Arvin, CA*

## The Soul Snake

Suppressing the darkness
Into the withering blackened soul
The slimy snake gets its feast
The snake grows with every hit
Every hit into the darkness
The darkness grows deeper
The snake grows longer
The soul gets blacker
Charred with smoke and flames
Releasing the slithering snake
To devour the being
Sucking out everything
Everything that lives
Leaving it only
With the crushed soul
Expanding darkness
Everywhere
Into everything
Every soul
Every snake
The world is left scorched
By the soul snake

Hunter Whitehouse
*Erie, CO*

## Estranged

Every one of us
Still around, but
Too far apart, Can't help it happened
Right from the start. We're
Abortive, inherited
Nature. Who's to blame?
God only knows. Born in a culture of
Emptiness. Always alone, and
Damn, always the same.

Jayme Chase
*Tumwater, WA*

## Him

As dawn approaches, outside's cold embrace tickles my skin. I feel the wind as it braids its way through my hair. My mind is racing like a million cars without a break. My cheeks are flushed pink thinking of him. him. him. He's somehow poisoned my mind with the scent that lingers when he leaves, the feeling that I know too well. His hands are inching their way down my body memorizing every bit. His lips are drinking in my lips and I'm gasping for a snap back into reality. Too afraid I might become trapped in his embrace. His eyes drowning in mine. I'm paralyzed. Unable to move or speak. Only think. think of him. him. him. A water droplet surprises my shoulder and suddenly the cars find their breaks.

Lindsay Copple
*Palm Beach Gardens, FL*

## Little Glass Bottle

Sometimes that little glass bottle makes me think.
What would I do without that little glass bottle?
How my muscles would quiver
How my skin would crack
And how my head would ache
How my feet would vibrate
How my nerves would succumb
How my blood vessels would collapse
How my kidneys would fail
And my spine twist
How my teeth would shake
How my heart would palpitate
And how my brain would dehydrate
My body would run itself into the ground...
just to keep living.
Wow.
I, and so many others, would be dead within days without our little glass bottles.
This isn't right, everyone should have the right to their own life.
Or at least the privilege of dying more slowly

Lucy Ensign
*Birmingham, AL*

*Hello, my name is Lucy Ensign. My poem is about the insulin affordability crisis in the United States. I am a type one diabetic and am passionate about this issue. I wish you the best of love, luck, and hope in all your endeavors!*

## Keep Them Coming Back

The sweet red lips keep them coming back
Even when their secrets loom across their shoulders
The clack of her 4 inch heels on payment
Oh yeah, that tight black dress will keep them coming back
The musk in the air was heavy when she was picked up in a silver Chevy
The boom of his voice was loud and familiar
His pores seeped out Bud Light and Miller
She couldn't see his face, but she knew it was something corrupt
He told her here they'll go back to his place
But the turns kept coming
He just went on hummin'
The headlights blinded her and the cars zoomed by
Oh my, oh my
She's starting to get anxious
He's starting to look suspicious reaching for his pocket
She needs to get out of the car, but he locked it
Her vision starts to fade and her head is a blaze
His eyes are wide filled with gore and pride
Her lungs gasp, reaching for something in a maze
His sweet lips are dripping red, it's what keeps them coming back

Riley Jackson
*Battle Creek, MI*

## 9-11

They stood grand
They stood tall
Until the day of 9-11 downfall
Loved and never forgotten one and all
We got blindsided our hearts hurt at what we saw
Some lost some
Most lost all
To every volunteer that came to our devastating call
God bless you everyone
God bless us all
You thought we was weak
You thought we was small
That was your greatest downfall
We stand United
We stand tall

Christopher Thomas
*New Matamoras, OH*

## Little

The incessant blows of
taken innocence of
teeth grinding of
nails, clenched hands
cut skin
tremors.
every day learning to re give that piece away,
every day learning to accept what grows in its place
(wave swell move, time-melting mist,
forwards- fervently kissing shore
... sometimes)
I sleep on shards of bones
and under the speculation of
ever really being home

Emily Shehee
*Temple City, CA*

## Shambles

I don't have a nickel
And I don't have a dime
But I can give you a tickle
And a really clever rhyme
I'm a little bit crazy
But I seem to get bye
I'm a little bit lazy
And sometimes I will lie
My dreams are often evil
As black as can be
And sometimes I often wonder
If the beast is after me.

Terry Oiler
*Springfield, OH*

## Anxiety

Sitting in my room rocking back and forth,
I can feel the monster called anxiety come forth.
It wraps its arms around me, not wanting to let go.
Only squeezing me tighter as it goes.
It's getting harder to breath, why won't it loosen up?
But I mustn't panic, I mustn't give up.
If I open my eyes, and look around, I can see I'm not stuck,
But have both my feet firmly on the ground.

Rebecca Eisel
*Lake Cyrstal, MN*

## Feel

The way you make me feel, you will never know. It's a feeling I can't explain, a unique blend of happiness and pain. Happy to have you, but pain because you aren't mine. I hate you but I love you. A divine twine in mind that relapse and runs its course. Jumping back into your sweet cloudy memories with no remorse, only sympathy from this perpetuous choice. Like are you trying to drive yourself crazy? Honey suckle berry Barb, he is nothing but a man and for that he leaves scars. Scars that only he can heal. The antidote the apology pill, he crosses his T's and dots his I's 'cause he's for real—gone hold you down like a sergeant you know the drill. But how long will it last before the past runs into them and crash? The agony of a cheap thrill, people forget what you've done for them but they will never forget how you made them feel!

Sade Yarbrough
*Tallahassee, FL*

## The Perfect Storm

How do you make the perfect storm?
How do you make a perfect piece of paper, if it's already torn?
Step One
You take the thunder and quaking of your heart, this is the perfect place to start.
Step Two
You take the lighting from your head,
the piercing yellow hue,
the quaking bolts of words that were never said.
Step three
Take the raindrops from your eyes,
you know the forgotten promises you use to treasure like a prize.
Pinch a cloud from your fantasies and add it to the mix,
you know from the daydreams that always made your heartbeat quick.
Take all the ingredients outside while the stars are aglow.
Close your eyes and dream about home.
Through the echo of the dew-covered grass, the ingredients will be reborn.
I am a cyclone of all the elements.
I am the perfect storm.

Cierra Calmeise
*Louisville, KY*

## Cold Hands

My hands are cold as they always are.
Cold hands to the touch,
usually people don't care for too much.
I never thought,
cold hands would be the only way she recognized me!
I lay my hands upon her head.
All the hair is gone; not even a thread,
this poem is for the twain that's dead.
Through the fever and the pain
she called out my name!
A sigh of comfort, a sigh of ease
who knew cold hands would please.
Another,
came in out of the cold, and did as I often do.
She said in a whisper,
"Squeaky is that you."

Lynette White
*Milwaukee, WI*

*I am an ordained minister, a fifty-one-year-old African-American woman. My greatest desire is to make a difference in this world. The poem "Cold Hands" was inspired at a time when my twin sister Yolanda White was dying from lung cancer. One evening at the hospital, the family surrounded her bedside while she lied on her death bed. My twin was in and out of consciousness but when I rubbed and soothed her head with my cold hands, she said with a weak voice, "Squeaky, is that you?" My twin was a beautiful soul.*

## A Love Poem (actually)

I need more pictures in my poems.
Like water strolling over stones.
A creak, in an old staircase.
Stepping, into a new perspective.
Looking at the words I write,
I want to see the thoughts behind them.
A writer, editor, and publisher, all in one.
Indeed a poem in progress.
You and I are one in the same,
Masterpiece in the making.
I hope you see what I am writing.
Do the words look pretty to you?
Like sunshine peaking through leaves.
Walking, along the beach alone.
Borrowing, body heat in the cold.
Expressing who I am, through who you are.
Analogies for what 'love' is.

Ellen Egeland
*Arlington, VA*

## Our Motherland

For what power has this motherland given us?
For which a battle has always been won
That offers our people protection when others are in a fuss
When my people first made contact with this soil
In the dawn of 1607 in Jamestown, Virginia
They were not one to struggle or spoil
What my people did was survive
Through those harsh winters
They bit their tongues and strived
In 1775, we wanted to be free
The UK was one to oppose
Then there was a war to be
Now there is a war still among us
Not with our guns but with words
They shout and they cuss
Whatever happened to our motherland?
She's beaten down by the jealousy of others
The one place that was so grand
These people look at me with hatred
Just as they would with a military man
I'm different now, a jingoistic girl
Who is only an American

Makenna Cuebas
*Wheeler, IN*

## Alien

Alien.
What could she mean?
Alien.
With skin so soft and certainly not green.
Alien.
That can't be right.
Alien.
This woman who sings to me at night?
Alien.
She? Who held me to her breast?
Alien.
Then sweetly laid me down to rest.
Alien.
This I can't believe.
Alien.
If true, then why would she leave?
Alien.
If that's her, then why not me?
Alien.
For she, anything I would be.
Alien.
This woman who above I would place no other.
Alien.
This warmth and comfort I call Mother.

Michelle Davick
*Fort Collins, CO*

## Pulchrum Visu Periculosa

We burn holes in the moon with our eyes
And we cause stars to go supernova
The sun clings to the sky by ties
But one day it will fall to Earth in a coma
It's impossible to focus on the dust in the air
Or the lines that make your fingertips unique
If I could see what I wanted, anywhere
I would set fire to every mountain peak
These particles that settle on my windowpane
Are made to simply emit energy
When my eyes fall, these particles don't stay
Committed to defying lethargy
Like the way the sun reflects on the leaves
These blades of green make a minefield of fire
The cause of destruction, a diamond, believed
My sight has trapped me in a flame roaring higher

Joanna Burt
*Rindge, NH*

*The words of a beautiful poem will come at the worst time. Perhaps it's at the end of third period when the chaos of packing up your things and lining up at the door shakes your brain just right, and the first line of young poetry is born. Or maybe they come at night when your focus is on the ceiling or the wall or the way your hand bends. It lights your mind and soon the lines are filled with words.*

## Hey Youngin, You Know I Went to High School With... NBA Legends

Anthony was called "the brow" his one defining feature
Bill was a real winner and wasn't afraid to remind you
Cleveland gave us Lebron, a special kid who moved out west but was never forgotten
Dirk never left his home, he preferred to fade away
Earvin didn't own a wand or rabbit, but still liked to perform magic
Fighting with Kevin wouldn't be wise. He was kind of crazy
Giannis was a skinny freshman, but after some years his strength was unmatched
Hakeem's moves were so swift and sweet, many girls called him dreamy
Isiah dated my sister's friend, she said she liked bad boys
James liked to cherish high school memories to take a step back and reflect
Kareem had big dreams, for him the sky was the limit
Larry was a simple man, He enjoyed working in the garden
Michael, to me was arrogant, he must have thought he was the greatest
Nikola was the class clown, and always filled the halls with laughter
Oscar wasn't a grouch, but always had a chip on his shoulder
Paul never told a lie, the most honest person I've ever met
Quiet Kawhi was almost robotic, but always got his work done
Russell always gave maximum effort, he never seemed to run out of energy
Steph liked to go hunting, he was a real sharp shooter
Tim had a summer job at the bank, and he didn't like to travel much
Unstoppable, that man Shaquille, he was a force to be reckoned with
Vince grew to be a star and he shined without any jewelry
Wilt had the school record for everything, some of them will never be broken
'Xceptional people like Kobe come once in a life time, the young kids would shout his name
Yao was the exchange student, but seemed to fit in pretty well
Zach wasn't as well known as the others, he always had his head in the clouds

Darian McGhee
*Silver Spring, MD*

## The Forgotten

I am the boarded-up house,
Left alone and abandoned.
I am the furniture,
Feigning dignity,
Cold stuffing bleeding over the dust.
I am the old broken floors,
Creaking in the wind,
And windows that cracked over and over and over again.
I am shattered beyond repair.
My walls are the faded blue of worn-out hopes
Lost and bleached by long years of sun
With black blotches of mold:
Scars from ancient rains.
The wood rots within and my shredded shades
Are drawn shut against the world,
To keep you from seeing the withered pain inside.
I stand as a reminder to those who remember
When all my friends stood
In endless ranks against the sunset.
I am the boarded-up house,
Dying on the lonely boulevard.

Erin Maas
*Atlanta, GA*

## Time

Time is the universe's sole rationality,
an infinite ticking clock that
cannot reverse,
will not reverse,
and impassive to those who attempt ignorance.

Time is the universe's sole enemy,
an unconquerable force with unfathomable fortifications,
impartial to the sinners,
the loved,
the strong,
the sickly,
collecting mindless souls
mindlessly in its endless wake.

Maggie Curtis
*Springfield, PA*

*Maggie is a tenth grade student at Springfield High School in Springfield, PA. She has been writing short stories and poems since she was a young girl. Maggie is also very committed to soccer, predominately playing in midfield positions. She lives with her parents and two younger sisters and the family dog.*

## Through the Motions

Something's coming over me, what's this emotion?
Is it love or lust
All I know is that it's strong like an explosion
Is it hate or fear
It's like I'm enchanted by the strongest potion
Is it happiness
Sometimes it pulls me under like waves in the ocean
Could it be sadness
All of these feelings seem to go unspoken
Maybe it's boredom
Maybe my brain just wants to cause commotion.
What if it's disgust
My head is scrambled so I take ibuprofen
My mind's like a rose
It may be pretty but the thorns leave me broken
Maybe it's calmness
And the silence is what's causing the bad omens
Then it is peaceful
But I'm still unsure of what my mind has chosen
I don't seem to know
What to do with myself I'm being woven
Into confusion
When I figure it out I'll take that token
In admiration
Because I survived going through the motions.

Sayler Smith
*Plain City, UT*

## Moonlight Rendezvous

Cow pastures stretch into the night sky.
Living a schedule all self-owned
Sneaking out into the chirping night,
Careful not to stir sleeping dogs
Or slumbering house members,
To rendezvous with who, too, knew
An undeniable love for the moon.
Alone in the dark, stars reflecting
Anger, sorrow, joy, companionship
Expelling from a mouth rarely opened,
Revealing secrets known by the one
Obsessive mind, one that can't let it
Go, the mind who loves the moon
To the point eye contact is fine.
Facing the shadowed craters face
Who listens to whispered confessions
Of over-thought wrongs, mistakes,
Questioning the path set forth,
With twists and turns and loops
Lessons learned, taught, in-progress
But also of love, relief, and pride
In family, friends, lovers missed,
Aged pets, kids, or memories cherished,
To the darkest depths of a living soul,
For the freedom, safety, comfort, release
Found in a moonlight rendezvous.

Samantha Sheffield
*Holts Summit, MO*

## The Pits of My Never-Ending Misery

I've have things that go out of my life, school
Why? You ask. Because I'm the owner of this despair and
I'm a one-time school student every ten years and a bum.
I'm a one time employee with no promotion and low pay.
Also, never-ending misery for me to be is a man without
A future. My life is in the dumps. I don't ask for much.
I just want the pits of my never-ending misery to end.
The pits are withdraws from three schools and a big
Stack of nonexistent employment history, I have there.
I have no skills to match, nothing to offer anyone.
My fantasy of hanging myself on a ceiling to end the
Pits of my never-ending misery is the only that
Satisfies me. I always thought being dead is better than
Being alive. I won't have to worry about nothing.
Thus, I try to be slick and make something of myself.
I end up doing nothing but failing: twenty years at
Home with no job, car, no apartment, no girlfriend,
No friends, no hopes for the future. This is my fate and
I accept it as such, for this is the pits of my never-ending
Misery.

Dwaun Marshall
*Chicago, IL*

## Fear

What have I done... he will know about it!
Should I lie and cover with deception?
I know not how he feels, no perception.
Nor to drinking today does he admit.
He is getting closer; I can feel him!
My legs are weakening; my mind, it throbs.
Perhaps I can plead through desperate sobs?
The aching of my heart fills to the brim.
He is here now, sudden as an earthquake.
He tells me I am worthless as I weep.
The sound rings loud as my heart and bones break.
The pain of his blows slow to a dull creep.
It leaves me to wonder if I shall wake,
But if he is there, I shall stay asleep.

Sadie Hanna
*Jackson, TN*

## Wasted

After the battle was over,
Amidst the remains of millions,
One figure was left alive.
A small boy, no more than seven,
Staring with wild eyes at the bones around him.
Having even lived through it,
He still could not comprehend such horrors.
How many, he wondered.
How many lost lives was he standing amongst?
Each of these bodies had a name.
A family.
A world.
Before it was all thrown away.
Tears dripped down his cheeks,
Washing away the blood on his hands.
They soaked his clothes,
Each tear a tribute to the fallen.
Wasted.
All of these souls,
Doomed to roam the battlefield for eternity.
And they didn't even win.

Corinne Murdock
*Columbus, OH*

## Ode to Father Mulcahy

I stood in line for lunch one day
At the mall in Century City.
Ahead, I heard a sound I knew,
The voice of Father Mulcahy.
Defrocked for years, still towhead blond,
The man I beheld was the actor
Who played a priest, or, priestly played,
Lending M*A*S*H its transcendent factor.
His falsetto tones took me back in time
To the best of TV, I am certain.
Yet, it struck me that day,
Has it ever struck you?
That he sounded like Thomas Merton!

Sheila M. Cronin
*Chicago, IL*

*Long ago I received a tape of a discussion led by Thomas Merton at the Abbott of Gethsemane. Recordings of his voice can easily be heard now but back then were rare. Years later while standing in line, nearby I heard the voice of William Christopher, the actor who had played a priest on M*A*S*H. The similarity between the famed monk's and character actor's voices inspired this poem. I am also the author of two novels: The Gift Counselor, winner of the Beverly Hills Book Award, and Best of All Gifts, the sequel.*

## Happy Doves

A dove sits on the roof and coos.
A nearby dove pretends to snooze.
She flirts, flitters, and flies away.
He chases her; he wants to play.
They fly up in a big tall tree
Where curious boys cannot see.
The next day they build a nest
Out of hay and all the rest.
On the third day little eggs sit
Under mother, warm woolen mitt.
Finally ends long, long wait,
(That, I assure you, all birds hate!)
Tiny little chicks finally emerge
And lovingly look at the two big birds.
Their mother smiles, their father grins.
They have something to take pride in,
That they chose life, because, you know, after all,
"A person's a person, no matter how small."

Faustina Darnowski
*Corydon, IN*

*I love to draw and to write poems, especially about birds. They are so fast, and I wish that I could fly. I like to play birds with my nine siblings, and sometimes it gets noisy so it's like being in a nest with little baby birds.*

## White Shells

The shoreline is littered with what were
once perfect white shells; all
that remain now are fragments of their
once perfect existence.
Though they are small, some so much
that they are almost missed
as they blend in with the surrounding sand, still have
sharp enough edges to break the skin.
The crisp sting seeps into the fresh cuts
as the salty waves rush the shore again,
you weren't careful enough.
The waves again recede back in the vast
ocean leaving behind their fragile, fresh
white shells. Perhaps
this time you shall tread more carefully.

Alicia Williams
*Craigsville, WV*

## Tomorrow

Yesterday, something lost and gone
Except for the knowledge
The dreams that night
The books read and
The friends made but,
Yesterday, is a day you can't get back.
Today, a present to all
Who awaken in a daze, or those who sleep
Take it as a gift
To explore, to dance
Today a gift from yesterday
Today a day left to fate.
Tomorrow, an illusion
A day that never comes
Only to be out of reach
Hope, for one day you will capture it
To the narrow valley that you find
Tomorrow is always Today.
So,
"Learn from yesterday,
Live today and
Hope for tomorrow" -Albert Einstein

Caleb Jones
*Longmont, CO*

*My real name is Elena Natasha Rodriguez. I wanted to use a pen name because this is my first time putting my work out into the world. I thought it would be neat to use another name but I realized it wasn't me. I wanted to recognize my grandma Karen and my best friend Anna for inspiring me to publish my work.*

## The Willow That Consumes

Watch the willow as you fade, my sweet,
Watch it sway as you do the same,
And let your heart skip those beats
When you lose thy mortal frame.
You can hear, my sweet, the sound of our mother
Hanging in the bows of the willow
She's also swinging limply under its cover
Her eyes as pearly white as your pillows
Cry like the bird in the parlor,
The men with crow's face are appearing soon
Your knight is coming to find the chip in his armor
Swallow it quick 'tis almost noon
I'll miss the laugh you left to echo in that hall
Unbeknownst to the horrors you left in the wake
Now the willow is sending me the call
No one will be left for the raven men to take
I'll bind the branches up above mother
So that they can't see my crimson rain
I know you're crying on the cloud, but do not bother
Watch the willow my sweet, for soon I'll see you again

Kate Richardson
*Los Altos, CA*

## #deep

I looked up and saw the moon
Bright and cheeky, a cheshire grin in d'skies
I wanted it to mean something but
It didn't
I looked down and saw a flower
Thin and delicate, a spiderweb bursting with dew
I wanted it to mean something but
It didn't
I looked out into the world
Loud and chaotic, a bazaar with more people than wares
I wanted it to mean something but
It didn't
I looked into myself
Too old and too young, a child burdened with license to adulthood
I wanted to mean something but
I don't
But whatever
Meaning is overrated

Salem Kowalski
*Bentonville, AR*

## I Mean

i love rainy days
and no,
i don't mean that like you're a rainy day
i mean that rainy days and monsoon seasons
were the only thing that kept me sane
i love rainy days
but i loved you, past tense,
staying in bed made more sense
when the sky was grey
thunder made my heart feel something
that wasn't just broken or empty or heavy
you held an umbrella over my heart
but it was already shriveled, too dry to function
a barely existent heartbeat
revived by lightning flashes
i love someone else
and so do you
and no,
i don't mean that like it's a bad thing
i mean that i wish you would have told me sooner
when your love left.

Grace Buckley
*Flagstaff, AZ*

## The Ascent

Life pulled the trigger, but the bullet missed.
It hit a mirror behind me whose glass shards pierced my body, and I wasn't facing the mirror so I didn't see it coming. As I removed each piece, I looked in the reflections and saw the different parts of me that needed to be healed; denial of being different, shame surrounding my life's path, fear of failure, loss and sorrow for the battles I have fought.
I took the bloody pieces and soaked them in a tub of salt water. Then I added some sweet smelling oils of empathy and compassion. I gently scrubbed those shards until they shined of strength and glistened with courage. I glued them back together and looked at myself in the mirror.
Facing forward I see myself looking strong. My eyes are deep and relaxed with a determined look. A slight smile rests on my face and I am standing tall. If I look closely I can see the scars, but only because I know where to look. I will look for them to remind me who I am when I get lost, to remind me of my resilience.
I continue to look at the mirror and my eyes settle on the cracks. It had broken, and it was beautiful.

Chloe Rasmuson
*Washington, DC*

## Winter's Befuddlement

And Winter sped along to Spring,
but weather is a fickle thing.
The seasons didn't seem to know
when rain should come and snow should go.
The air was tasteless when the Lamb
lay with the Lion for a fleeting span.
Together they played in the field,
for all the greater Nature's yield.
But storms of hail did snuff their fun,
and the time of growing had come undone.
But this was not the proper fit
for a brand new Spring, bright lit.
The Lion made a terrible roar
that should have been a rumbling snore,
and the Lamb let loose a garbled lament
which only gentle sunshine could prevent.
Yet still a confused Winter's tizzy rained
and pelted ice 'til the ground was pained.
It's oft' not useful to resist
the wrath of Heaven's laundry list,
no matter how inane.

Sadee Ferres
*Worcester, MA*

## Syd

Your own hallowed existence,
a dimension, cold and hollowed by reckless wandering,
in search of forgetting what you can't understand
Still remembered,
and now gone.
Bits and fragments of children songs surface
through the haze,
harboring sympathy in an intense state of being
Eclipsed by darkness and rhapsodized on the moon,
you become lost in the differences
that are lingering
within
Sensationalized as a prophet in documents
that are heard everywhere.
A lost and lonely angel
on the verge of enlightenment but
falling
in your own black abyss.

Joshua Murray
*Jonesboro, IL*

## Dreaming

Have you ever dreamed of springtime
With its beauty so bold and free?
Have you ever sensed the freshness
Which flows from a rolling sea?
Have you ever watched the moon at night
So distant with splendor it seems?
Have you ever felt this good in life?
Does it enter in your dreams?
These things are all around us,
But to most they're not the same.
Yet, to find this peace and happiness
Is what I call my aim.
This is the way I see you,
As I dream throughout each night.
God gave the world this beauty to see,
Enriched by you, the soul of my sight.

James Campbell
*Chesnee, SC*

*I started writing poetry in the sixties; much of it related to the face of a lady I often dreamed about but never met. I would wake up in the morning and couldn't wait to sit down and start writing about this lady. I did this for over thirty years until one day I met a beautiful lady at work and realized she was the face in my dreams. Immediate love was mutual, the dreams ceased, and she is now my wife forever. I wrote the poem "Dreaming" for our wedding invitations.*

## Rain Man

I can't stand waiting in the rain
For some reason it causes discomfort in my brain
But there is a funny thing about water from the sky
Somehow people can't handle the wet and must be dry
Yet we bathe and shower almost every day or more
But then we are in control over that cleansing pour
We are completely calm in our homemade storm
Yet put me in a drizzle and watch the anxiety form
The rain brings us water for all of life's thirst
And yet it's a bother because our comfort comes first
I think we hate rain because it's out of our reach
It comes when it wants no matter what we preach
Rain is nature's reminder we don't have all the power
So let the drops fall and appreciate God's shower

Adam Spaulding
*Wabash, IN*

*Greeting, poetry lovers! My name is Adam Spaulding. I am eighteen years old and attend Purdue University. I have been writing poetry often during the last few months. My poem "Rain Man" was inspired by the movie Rain Man, featuring Tom Cruise and Dustin Hoffman. I started thinking about a certain scene in the movie where Raymond refuses to go outside because it is raining. That got me thinking about why rain is so uncomfortable and often annoying when, if you think about it, it brings life to everything.*

## The Pause

Deafness in tones of silver struck my face and body
Cold and frigid stillness as I lay in the first snowfall.
Death no longer lingered nor the wilds of nature
Coming all to see the process at its' working peak.
They let it be known here and afar
As if their own had fallen past life's point.
Sending cries of no words but plenty of love
Now understanding I too was a part of them.
Breathless as the heartbeats slowly drifted away
All the lights of the universes halted.
Blackness crept its way through gently
My soul then road on the winds of time.
No longer bound to my undoing wounds
From man's destructively hopeful dreams.
Free of every ill and deceiving truths
Nothing is more powerful than the edge of everywhere.

Jodi Arroyo
*Spokane Valley, WA*

## Cherished by One

When you are old and grey,
Wrinkled and too tired to play,
Sit back, stretch by the old fireplace,
Pull up the crimson blanket to your face.
And know that many swooned over your looks,
They loved your money, and the dazzling rocks.
They craved your story, and all the medley,
And they cheered you on, clapping wildly.
And then know that there was one who wished you ugly,
Someone who wished you possessed not a penny.
Who cared not for a tale so fancy,
And hated everything that ruined your true beauty.
Who would have stayed true, if the face had faded,
And would have starved, had the luck grown jaded.
Who wished that all that remained was simple trust,
To fall back on, when everything else went bust.
Yet, looks came cheap, money aplenty,
The follies of youthfulness grew trendy.
Playing at royalty, cracking down,
Wrecking the purity, with the cruelest frown.
So when old and grey, you turn,
And for the fleeting memories, you yearn,
Know that you were loved by many,
But also know that you were truly cherished by one.

Tina Sebastian
*Lewis Center, OH*

*I am a software engineer by day and a poet by night. I live in Columbia, OH, with my husband and our five-year-old preschooler twins. Writing and reading poetry is a welcome break from the daily hustle and bustle of raising kids and working. Poetry is my form of relaxation, an avenue to express my feelings without the lingering regrets. My poems are usually a depiction of events and people from my life. "Cherished by One" is a portrait of a dear friend who has had several admirers over the years and an accompanying message to remember that no matter what hardships may befall, there would always have been that one person who cherished them for the right reasons till the end.*

## Falling Figures

The image is burned into my memory. It stains my mind like day-old coffee split on a brand new white wedding dress. I see it every time I close my eyes. I see... Them. All those blurry shadows. I see all those shadows falling at a ungodly speed. They looked like rag dolls as they fell, surrounded by a thick cloud of thick grey smoke and pieces of falling debris. The ground on which they landed was engulfed in roaring red angry flames. I heard the screams of other bystanders. Hundreds of screams became one otherworldly howl. People were running all around me while I stood in the middle of the street staring up at the black smoke filled sky. Someone grabbed my arm and tried to get me to move but I couldn't move, I didn't move , I wouldn't move. More shadows fell from the sky into the red fire. Off in the distance there was a low rumble then a BANG! I fell to the pavement, covered my head and closed my eyes, and waited for something. What I was waiting for, to this day I still don't know. Maybe I was hoping that today didn't happen, or hoping that I didn't witness human beings jumping off the Twin Towers. That day stained my mind and it stained our nation.

Emily Sax
*Woodbridge, CT*

## Haunted Heart

Too far gone no love
He's filled with an intense rage
Only the repetitive familiarity of his dark lonely cage
Hours go by days of his insanity grows
His thoughts of the one true woman
He always loved betrayed and left for dead this she knows
Beautiful images of her keep replaying in his mind
If only they could restart and rewind
Will he ever love another the same way he used to love
That old hurt and heavy weight pounds in his chest
The old familiar ache he crumbles and starts to shake
Thoughts running wild and a mess how did I ever get
Far he tries to cry but he can't another night walking
A lonely mile to the bar he realizes the weight of his
Own heart he cannot and will not find his random
Recollections begin to torment and haunt his mind
The girl he used to come home to so happy to see
In one brief moment she feels haunted by his ghostly memory

Marie Demerell
*Gaylord, MI*

## Memory Burn

you did not leave it only him, not only him, us
and empty you did give us empty
but fear belongs to you so you packed it next to the photo albums that
were not yours i'm surprised there was room for it i'm surprised
the offence wasn't personal i know, but it was moral in nature and
now i don't believe in anything
my friends' mothers raised me and i still can't
look them in the eye because you never taught me how
to love a woman in myself or in others
i searched for years before learning that the wrong places even existed
and now i am still trying to climb back out i am exhausted
i would never forgive you
i would never forgive you and
i did but i would never
sometimes i feel gutted with guilt for feeling and thats when i resent
you
the most for never teaching me to be sure and sometimes i feel grateful
for my capacity to love but mostly i feel alone
and somehow at rest, it's evident now that the moon was always there
even when i couldn't reach her and no i am not talking about you

Nathalie Chazoule
*New York, NY*

## Pain

What can this pain be, that hides in my chest?
What can this pain be, that gives me no rest?
This pain that I feel, lies deep within my heart;
it sometimes feels like, it's ripping me apart.
Oh what can this pain be, that refuses to see;
the devastating effects, it's having on me.
This pain is sporadic, for it comes and goes.
Sneaking up on you, as though it were your foe.
This pain resembles a coward,
striking when you're weak.
Reducing you to tears, with feelings that are bleak.
This pain is full of meaning,
its purpose, meant to be grasped.
In order for you to attain it,
this pain puts on a mask.
It does not mean to hurt you,
but it knows no other way;
of making you understand, what it's trying to convey.
This pain will have no pity, when trying to express,
the vast, empty feeling in you, this pain called
Loneliness.

Yvonne Evans
*Hesperia, CA*

## Onward

Onward and upward you go
I will mourn the coming days without your voice
Feel peace in the embrace
of those who've gone before
For you to stay here, there was no choice
Onward and upward you had to leave
I will mourn the days gone by and memories shared
Find peace at last; Rest well my friend
In the forest, there's no need to be scared
Onward and upward, finally free
I will mourn but not long; I will try
For your body has gone, yet you still live on
Only the physical you said good-bye
Onward and upward;
Look after me, my friend
As I will remember you throughout remaining hours
You have not died
You have not left
In the forest you've become the flowers
Onward and upward you go
Now growing as a flower, colourful and bright
Casting beauty over dark forest floors
Bringing brightness to dark gloom's night
Onward and upward you go,rest well
I will mourn the coming days without you by
You,
now a Flower of the Forest, my friend
Will be watered from the tears I must cry

Myke Eggers
*Orlando, FL*

## A Difference

A single act can make
a difference.
A single word can make
a difference.
A single gift can make
a difference.
A single friend can make
a difference.
We Can All
Make
A
Difference
So,
Why,
Don't,
We?

Zach Doering
*Alleman, IA*

## Nature's Course

For days he sought
my Promised Land.
Plundering -
pounding between
my mountains thighs,
gleaming
with silver ridged
stretch marks.
I surrendered -
a screaming gale!
He finished his quest
a victor.
Beneath the moon
night terrors shook
my sweat slick body.
He left behind
the stain of Man -
a parasite to grow
as promised.

Christine Zielinski
*East Brunswick, NJ*

## Mask

She hides behind a mask so no one can see
She is fighting a battle internally
It beats It bruises It makes her cry
And in the end, all it tells her is lies
She lies in bed trying to sleep
But all she hears is defeat
She cries and cries and cries some more
Because inside is a war
You don't see how she feels
Because with her mask on she can conceal
She fights with her head
To smile and laugh
So no one can see what's behind her mask
What you see is a happy smile
When inside is pretty vile
She hates that she is hiding who she is
But to her, it is better than to know what you think of who she is
She is lost
But again you'll never know
Because she puts on her mask
Hides her feelings and puts on a show

Karina Schaeffer
*Carson, WA*

## Death of a Friend

my chest was ripped open
my heart thrown to the ocean
left to drift a million miles away from my mind
the raw pain of eternity
stings my eyes and squeezes my lungs
until
i'm left lying on the ocean floor
desperately searching for what is no more

Makena Caron
*Hadley, MA*

## A Recipe for Fall

One cup of falling leaves
Swaying in the air
Two pints changing leaves
colorful in the sky
Five pounds of pumpkin patches
Filled with fat pumpkins
One teaspoon houses all decorated for Halloween
With webs, skeletons, and Jack-O-Lanterns
Four dashes of trees
With different colored leaves filling the branches
Ten teaspoons of crispy air
Sting children's faces to make them rosey

Sophia Garrett
*Rogers, AR*

**Black Swan**

Time has passed
But not much has changed
These thoughts have harassed
And made me enraged
They go round and round
And seem to prevail
The thoughts and the sound
I continue to wail
The meds may diminish
The meds may aid
They say I should finish
But I still feel afraid
Nowhere to flee
Nowhere to hide
But to its decree
I just sit back and ride
With little control
I try to go on
Inside this dark hole
I wait for the next black swan

Emily Norton
*Mount Washington, KY*

## Sleeping Dream

Wind whistling into a lifeless night
When the moon shines full its sea-foam light
No singing of birds, nor howling of wolves
Dare summon ripples upon fate's pool
The woods are still and remain like so
Unchanged by silence, or the distant glow
For none can break through this one wall
Unless a ghost within it all
If only the lake of dreams would sway
Rather than mirror a moonlit ray
Then I could sleep, embraced by the mist
Blanketed by that single gift
Many pale eyes gaze through this flesh
A hatchling separated from its nest
By little bits of shattered glass
The looming fog does humbly pass
Shadows gather where a meadow weeps
Shade finds no rest where two tears meet
Blind, yet blessed with the clearest sight
A single shard, a star painted white

Erin Gonzalez
*Madison, AL*

## The Weed

Hiding and reserved, the weed
Takes her place among the flowers.
Frightened, she tries to communicate
Yet, they react with equal fear.
She, faking verdure, ruffled her
Yellow, gaudy costume and stood taller.
The flowers reacted with fragrant curses,
Shrinking and flying into the soil & sky.
Timid or confident, the weed was alone.
Bitter and worthless, the weed sat waiting.
No blooming transformed her
And no animal wanted her.
Desperate, she spread out and grew
Until, finally, she was noticed.
A giant approached and looked at her,
Touched her, made her feel wanted with water and light.
After this initial affection, the
Goliath came up to her with a bottle,
Giving her a kind of love never before experienced-
A sensation of burning and fire and stinging
And
She never had the chance to love again.

Adelia Nunn
*Buckley, WA*

## Watchful Sun

The eye of dawn opens.
Its light spills across the world,
Like thoughts spilling across a newly awoken mind.
Cloudy eyelashes decorate the sun
Reflecting it beauty and color.
But still can they dull its shine,
Overcast and grey, the light is diminished
Like vacant eye sockets in the throes of grief and sorrow.
Soon follows a thunderstorm of tears
Soaking its world in the strength of its tenderness,
Before once again emerging anew, clear and focused.
Acting as our window to the universe
So do they also reflect the core.
On continues the cycle as the darkness of sleep creeps across the sky
Letting the sunlight sleepily fade away.
Only twinkling, starry dreams left
To be recalled in a sea of inky rest.

Alexandra Owsiany
*McMurray, PA*

## 16,000 Tears

16,000 natives
Of American land removed
From home and peace
Love and sleep
With nothing left to do
Babies crying
Children dying
We've stripped away their light
5043 miles of pain
And no more strength to fight
Ruthless dreams, and spewing lies
We have come to be
A newborn nation
Yes we are, but violence was the key
No consideration, of what they would have thought
The only thought was for "our nation"
Yet leaving them distraught
They may not be as evolved
But they are citizens, with a cause
Stripped away their culture
Stripped their friends
Stripped away their happiness
Kicked them off their land
16,000 tears
Dripping on the rocks
Walking on and on forever, shackled by their locks

Madeleine Braley
*Fairfield, CT*

## L.o.v.e

Love is as quick as snow...
Its grasp on your heart feels out of control
When your born it's the first thing you know
When you find the one and you never want to let go
When you have to hang up the phone and it hurts you so
Looking in their eyes makes a ting light glow
You notice the little things like when their hair starts to grow
Or when the curls in their hair starts to show
When you know that they love you so
Just know if it's  true love it will never go
The beats in your heart get a little louder
When his family looks at him they look a little prouder
The time when you saw sugar fall from his head like powder
Wow wild things aren't we
I love seeing him smile when he sees me
Or feeling his heart beat when we're clingy
It makes my heart a little more gleamy
The first time you met and he called you cute
I swear love will put the whole world on mute,
Yea I'm young I know I am, but I'm just so in love with him.

Taliyah Worsley
*Bear, DE*

**Follow Your Dream**

Always follow your dream
your heart is always right
no matter how hard it might seem.
Treat your ambitions with esteem
when you get lost in the night
always follow your dream.
Your hopes are supreme
never lose sight
no matter how hard it might seem.
As you watch your desires gleam…
do not fright
always follow your dream.
Your passions have burst through the seam
fulfill them with all of your might
no matter how hard it might seem.
A new day will arrive, and in the sun shall stream
for love is the light
always follow your dream
no matter how hard it might seem.

Stefani Haus
*Ankeny, IA*

## Teacher's Pain

Why feel?
Why shove a burden on another's chest?
Why assign them with an obligation
To multiply emotions for you
When you know that they're not sincere?
When one friend will suffocate you
At a moment when you have to beg for solitude,
One friend will shrink your concerns to dust
And claim deafening pep talks are the ideal broom,
And one friend will switch on a heart attack
From the fear of your cloudy days darkening,
Can you really blame me for pretending I feel less than Captain Holt
And weakening the threads between me and my family
While drowning in my tear-soaked pillow
Never feels as good as hugs they exchange?
If I ever unlock my heart, either pride will possess them
And stab me with "I told you so's"
Or I'm labeled as a snake in teacher's clothing
Until he spotlights himself in the background
And I sink into my paperwork-filled casket
Before they could feign guilt and apologies.
No matter what happens, I will always come back.
Despite all who mute my contributions, one person needs me,
But even he thinks being less me
Would bring more peace to his head.
I stare out at the sea like I just walked into a majestic painting.
I'll never be completely gone. I can never truly escape.

Monique Blackwell
*Bellwood, IL*

## When We Were Kids

when we were kids
we thought 60 watts would keep the monsters away
Mom and Dad would fight the day time monsters
how did we know?
we knew because they'd come home tired
we had to grow up fast.
Mom and Dad aren't here anymore
the demons gave them poison
replaced them.
when we were kids
we tied our toys with ropes
breaking them free, pretending to be heroes
now, we step on that chair, our last step to freedom
we hold that rope thinking
'this will set me free'
as we put on the rough necklace
we smile sadly as we think of Mom and Dad
but,
that was when
we were kids.

Alyssa Madsen
*Vancouver, WA*

## We Are Woman, Hear Us Roar

We wear our scars on our hearts for they make us who we are.
We get strength from our wounds given since leaving our mother's womb.
We are sister, aunt, niece, mother, lover and friend.
We hold each one beloved; we love them to the end.
We beat the soil beneath our feet until they're bloody and sore.
We are woman, hear us roar.
You can tell us that we're ugly, that we'll never get too far.
You can try to keep us in the dark,but we burn like the brightest star.
And when you try to throw us down, and push us in the dirt;
don't you know we grow stronger with every little hurt.
So until you realize what we are really for,
We are woman, Hear us roar.
We hold the very fabric of mankind in our hands.
So isn't it about time then,
they listen to our commands.
We will no longer stand to be
abused, raped and slaughtered.
We will chose to be accountable, and love what we have fathered.
We will no longer be silenced,
and tethered to the floor.
We will not deal in double standards and inequality like generations before.
And every time we put our feet down, our daughters: they will soar.
Because we stood our ever loving ground.
We are Woman, Hear us Roar!!!

Stephenie Yates
*Medford, OR*

## Reflection of My Thoughts Pt. 2

Whatever's in your heart
Just let it flow
Whatever's on your mind
Just let it go
We were ment to transcend
Increase our energy and high frequencies
I'm finding ways to articulate your mind
I got that automatic high
Feel like I can touch the sky
My life is like an open book
First ten chapters would probably
Have you shook
Broken clocks
And kisses of betrayal
Kinda felt like I was close to hell
Never understood why my life was so frail
Had to learn to let go and find myself
Had to kill the old me
Rebirth myself
Haven't been the same
Since I choose myself
Bought silence to the violence that I've
Once arrayed
Inspire
My honor
This is dedicated
to the peace and pain

Sakiyna Jones
*Fairview Park, OH*

## White Feather

White Feather, Indian squaw,
eyes a sot brown hue
against the moon and the desert stars.
White Feather, your beauty enchants me.
It captures my heart.
So deep I want to shout "Out loud!"

But oh White Feather,
now I must leave.
For nature calls.
And this desert that surrounds you...
Well, it isn't mine at all.
Because I am a white man
bound to only white women squaws.
And should a child be born a half breed?
He would hardly be free to roam.
He'd be shunned by the Indian nation
while the white man cursed him
and cast the first stone.

Suzanne Soucy
*San Jose, CA*

## Syncope

Falling freely
Light loving limbs
Listing toward heaven leaf heavy
Giants looming large who wisely
Breathe
Out what is needed
Taking in what's been exceeded
Breaking speed yet ever seeding
Life
Repeating over nature's cycle
Catching fools who've
Lost perspective
Lost consciousness
and vision
Embracing cataclysmic
new age thinking
Without complaining
Halt the faint heart
Heal with precision
Like Phoenix have arisen
Generation to generation
To be inspiration
Reminders-To recall
Hoping to prevent others' fall them.

Betty Hatfield
*Louisville, KY*

*I have been writing my own poems since I was five years old. I am now a retired nurse after forty-three years in the medical field. I have been married for forty-three and a half years to my brilliant, loving husband Paul, and we have three grown daughters, five spectacular grandchildren. I have currently been offered to make one of my poems into lyrics for a song from a company in Nashville, TN, where I attended college and met my husband. My family is very close. I have two older brothers who live in our home state of Georgia. Our visits are not often but filled with great times, laughs, and shared memories. My husband's family is also close. We have one living parent among us, Paul's mother, who is such a lovely, God-fearing prayer warrior. All in all I am blessed beyond measure and thankful to God for all His many blessings. His name be praised forever.*

## Stammer

leaf litter in the corridor,
stained purple glass
crushed underfoot.
velvet cloaks and,
saccharine syrup coating,
sticky to the touch.
marble finish and
silver fixtures
sulking in their iron rust,
to fresh cuts on raw knees.
dirty glitter-bleeding heart
ruining the floors.
and yet,
the sun rests on my skin,
and the air buzzes around me.
all of my strings are still strung too tight
my pitch strained,
out of tune.
arms outstretched in a first arabesque
waiting for an entrance.
worms roil and leaves rot.
how close to mush we all are
an inch away from mush we all are.

Merritt Snider
*Smyrna, GA*

## Shimmering Undertones of a Moth

picturing attachment to a pair of wings,
unnoticed in liberty,
feeling unsought in the air;
until the descent.

what is there to see
with only two hues:
a negative brilliance
a positive dimness.
what is there to feel
in the rest of the day,
when night is made
sorrowful for the remainder.
what is it to hear
what's supposed to be right
but, is only what's left
to be said from the past.
what is it to rise . . .
while being oblivious,
only to find
that it all was a ruse . . .

Carl E. Webb II
*Mesquite, TX*

## Love Out Loud

To be loved, should shine
like a bright sunny day,
In the month of May.
Inhaling the fragrance of life
as it passes away.
Love Out Loud !
Gently caress my carmel to dark brown skin,
never to forget where happiness starts
and true love begins.
Love Out Loud!
A chain that's unbreakable
a limb that will bend,but never break
only to regain it's strength, and stand
strong again.
Love Out Loud!
Being proud to wipe the sweat from your brow.
creating a piece of art, the greatest
gift of all, a caring heart
Love Out Loud!

Minnie Westbrook
*Cordova, TN*

## Life

Life is a game
Everyone plays,
Each battle is different
Each day is the same.
We pretend were all strong
And there's nothing wrong,
And the lessons we learn
Are just part of the song.
We act like it's normal,
We act like we're great,
But deep down inside we all hold our mistakes.
And just when you think the battle is won.
The game makes you realize it'll never be done.

Brandy Mohar
*El Paso, TX*

*I am a wife and mom of five kiddos. My family constantly tries to push me to my limits. I wasn't going to enter because I suffer from a lack of confidence and very bad grammar, but I am lucky enough to say I had a guardian angel who believed in me and a friend who pushed me. And all I can say is thank you to all of them for making my dream of being heard come true.*

## On Top of the World

He stands tall and proud,
his peak white with snow.
Rising above the highest cloud,
the valley, far below.
At the top, it is quiet,
quiet as the night.
His peak stands relient-
The noise can't reach his height.
The sun, moon, and stars
for him, he can always see.
Even the ones afar,
his view the best it can be.
The thought of this is very low-
that eventually this could all die.
No matter what, though,
he is always reaching high.

Chester Chestnut
*Ankeny, IA*

**Different Side**

There is a different side to everyone you meet. Some are good and some are harmful.
For you have a different side, a side that is hard to uncover, only few can uncover that side and learn what you are.
There are very little people like you in this world, kind, caring, and pretty. As I have learned over the years there are very few people in this world who are special, who share things that we have experienced, those people we must cherish and care for.
Life is short but if you live it right, it will have been all worth while. You shall experience great amounts of fear, happiness, sadness. But it is your decision on whether you take it as a lesson were you take the test and learn the lesson after.
For you have only begun your life as you grow, you will cherish the little things in life and grow from them.
The people you meet will have different sides, some will be good, some will be harmful. Your soul will guide you through the worst in days, just keep faith.
Because there is more to you than meets the eye.

Kendra Bell
*Cleveland, UT*

## Dancing in the Dark

One, two, three in the dark
Feel the beating of my heart
Dancing to a deadly tune
Swimming in the afternoon
Four, five, six your hand in mine
Feel the drum of ticking time
This dizzy beat we'll learn to handle
Swaying like a burning candle
Seven, eight, nine pairs of feet
Spinning in the summer heat
Dancing in the dark in tandem
I an angel and you the phantom
One, two, three in the dark
Hear the burning of my heart
In a room of quiet hollow
And a world of shifting shadow

Xavier Pimentel
*Spring, TX*

## Black Bird Code

black birds in formation
line the wires from pole to pole
avian symbols of morse code
bird bird bird dash
bird dash bird is it a great day for moving South
was it spread by bird or mouth
black birds in formation
lining the wires from pole to pole

Rex Seigler
*Wichita Falls, TX*

## Hear Me

Why can they not hear me?
I am desperately screaming below
I force air out, as my lungs fill with water
My voice is hoarse, Muddy and drowned out
But when I silence
They feel no difference
For a scream from my voice
Is but a whisper to their ears
Why can they learn?
To hear and recognize my pleas
When can they finally
Cater to me?

Laurissa Larimer
*Portland, OR*

## I Am Alone

I sit here alone,
Alone once again in the dark.
I'm now leaving more than just one mark
The blood is dripping,
Flowing with pain
Flowing with anxiety, depression and vain.
I try to lay, and cry myself to sleep
I have nothing happy in my mind to keep
Nothing keeping me away from suicidal thoughts.
Parting me from the fake people I've met.
There was a lot.
A lot of people who raised my fears.
A lot of people that made me cry
A lot of people who've made my personality dry.
I try to stop crying, I try, and I try
All I think about now is how much I want to die.
I then sit up
Thinking I might erupt.
Erupt of the anger, sadness, fear left behind
Realizing now I only have one thing left in mind.
I am alone.

Baily Carpinelli
*Aurora, CO*

## Wedding Day

Affection wins
Forgiven for our sins
Freshly baptized
Our love surmised
Cameras shutter
People mutter
A musical symphony
Guests on the balcony

Chest pounding
Pastor founding
Tummy's fluttering
He's stuttering
Tears in eyes
Dad's being wise
Everyone lingers
Rings on our fingers

Jump in the car
Honey, we're going far
To love and to cherish
Home is refurnished
In sickness and in health
With or without wealth
Till death do us part,
You'll always have my heart

Jennifer Lesko
*Torrance, CA*

## New Smiles

This year I felt scared,
Scared of letting what I had drift into the unknown
But when I finally loosened my grasp,
What I found was peace on one's own
And I'm writing to tell you that it's okay to lose hold
For letting go of some things will bring you closer to home
And home is not a building
But a place we like to go to feel less alone
So be but thankful when the years force you to say goodbye
For old soil brings new life
And long sorrow brings new smiles

Lauren Sturgeon
*Virginia Beach, VA*

*I wrote this poem while laying in my bed one night. I couldn't sleep but had an itch to write. I ended up writing this poem and it has become my favorite that I've written. I'm telling you this to say—always pursue what you love. Broken minds create beauty.*

## I Watch

I watched him.
The world graciously stopped moving so I could
Watch him.
My mother became victim to my father's hand.
He knocks her to the ground and I hear the smack so perfectly.
The sound echoes throughout the room and all around my mind.
He drags her by her hair,
Her long, soft brown hair,
And I watch as it becomes trapped within his fingers.
Her beautiful green eyes,
Turn dark and filled with blood.
They widen and close softly.
She knows she has lost again.
The more my mother cries for help,
The more useless and numb I become.
But all I do is watch,
As his hand breaks their vows
and my mother's nose.
And when he's done he walks, triumphantly,
Rewarding himself with a cold beer.
My mother lays in pain and defeated.
She sheds a single tear,
and I watch as it runs down her beautiful bruised face.

Ariana Garcia
*Moreno Valley, CA*

## Fine China

With just dust and a rib, I was created
My Lord molded me, and it was personal
Every flaw, intentional
Every gift, purposeful
You look at me and all my negative you may want to mention
Yet and still my soul is the Lord's, He holds all retention
The walk isn't easy, but I will be finished to completion
A lump of clay going through the fires
I'm letting Him do as He desires
Going through the furnace
It's nothing minor
On the other end I will be uniquely painted in spiritual gifts
Glory to the Lord for making this divine shift
You are really looking at fine china
I count it joy to be touched by The Potter's hand
With faith of a mustard seed I will make it to the Promise Land

Jessica Webster
*Aberdeen, MD*

## Sickly Mad Bird

Sickly mad bird, curled up in a jar
The powers above don't know about me
Trust that I'll guide you without interference
As you broaden your wings of absurdity
Sickly mad bird, I'll watch from afar
The flowers below don't blossom for me
Trust that I'll guide you to relish your brilliance
So fly little bird, through the forest of trees
Sickly mad bird, your moment has come
The night of your death is set to begin
You've been here before; I'll help you remember
The man you'll grow into, the same one you've been
Sickly mad bird, look what you've become
Your feathers have fallen, revealing your skin
The farther you go, I hope you'll remember
Your feathers embroidered with virtue and sin
Sickly mad bird, you're finally free
Gone forward and back, yet still in one place
I'm beckoned away, another young bird
With perils abound, the same ones you have faced
Sickly mad bird, a moment in time
What is and is not between you have traced
Perhaps you'll share with another young bird
That personal moment that can't be erased

John-Luke Pollock
*Newnan, GA*

## The Clouds

The clouds swirl into a multitude of shapes,
None of which can be certain.
Always changing and curling around each other,
Wondering what to do next.
Faces, sometimes animals, but never the same.
The elusive white wisps flutter about
Then disappear,
As fleeting as thought.

Emily Reiter
*Gardner, KS*

## The Pearl Earrings

I wear pearl earrings with a pleasant smile and a quiet demeanor.
This maintains a sense of purity and dignity.
So I take off the pearl earrings before going into his house.
It was time to drop the façade.
I leave his house with a lump in my throat, stench on my skin,
grease in my hair, and smeared eye makeup.
So I drive home and put on the pearl earrings from before.
The dark circles around my eyes and the bright pearls do not match in meaning.
So why is it that I am so confused?
Today, I kept the pearls on. Are they tainted or I am regaining my dignity?

Ashley Saathoff
*Kingman, AZ*

## Our Love

From the love we share
Our bodies shake and shiver
And keep each other warm

John Benson
*Sanford, NC*

## The Creation

We melted together there on that floor.
In that moment, time ceased to exist,
and neither of us needed anything more.
An entire universe existed only of our two bodies.
Galaxies formed,
falling from our lips.

Jordyn Christmas
*Elgin, OK*

## Dear Momma

Momma you gave life to me from a baby to a young lady
Momma you taught me how be strong in life and so much
more. There is no love like a mother's love.

Brittany Domenico
*Welsh, LA*

## Mama

Dear Mama
Thanks for this gift called life
You cut me so deep all I do is write
Only way to escape the pain
Yet I see those ugly scars remain
They constantly throwing dirt on my name
Trying to put me in the grave
Dear mama
Why did you have to do us like that
Just up and left and never looked back
Fast track years later
You were never sober
Our relationship is over
Your heart is growing colder and I'm getting older
Dear mama
I bet it hurts to see how I feel about you
At the end of the day you're always worried about you

Jessica Roman
*Tallahasse, FL*

## Sold-Out Show

As I look out,
Into the sold out crowd,
My knees begin to tremble,
And my head falls down.
The audience hates me,
I'm never quite good enough.
But I'm here against my will,
And I'll be back tomorrow.
In fact, I'll be back the next day too,
The day after that, and the next one too.
There's no escaping this crowd,
I'm stuck on this stage,
Day after day,
There's no way to escape.
Their heckles and boos,
Didn't bother me at first,
But after awhile, it started to burn.
My skins been removed,
My bones have been broken,
They've taken my soul,
Leaving me hopeless.
I just want to go home,
But I don't where home is.
The audience isn't real,
And neither is the stage,
This is just my life,
With the voices of my brain.

Brogan Thorstad
*Fargo, ND*

## The Little Girl Who Loves Christmas Too Much

There was once a girl who loved Christmas
But for her Christmas time was pure bliss
She loves wearing red
But when it was time for bed
She always wears green
When she went to school the other girls were being mean
She had a beautiful and sparkly tree
But when she was three
Her parents divorced and took the tree
But that wasn't the end
Because her Christmas spirit didn't bend
Her Christmas spirit might be broken
But that wasn't the end
Because that little girl was me
The end

Sophia Schoonveld
*Akron, MI*

## Love the Addict, Hate the Addiction

The day you left
You broke my heart
What I thought was the end
Was just the start
The start of grief
Everlasting pain
I thought it was over
But you left a stain
A stain on my heart
Seeping deep into my soul
Just when I thought it would stop
It turned my heart to coal
I lost all my faith
The unknown was known
Your actions were clear
Intentions were shown
I am your daughter
Everyday I'm sad
Because even though you're my father
You're a very bad dad
I've been told to love the addict
Only hate the addiction
But it's so hard to love you
Just look at your conviction

Jewelien McClure
*Sedro-Woolley, WA*

## Purpose

What is my purpose in life?
Do I go through life wondering if I should fall in line,
or do I wonder if I should take the lead?
How am I to know anything if I'm pushed into the mud,
constantly wondering if I'm good enough?
Who would tell me if my path is good, or bad,
or even if it was the right one to begin with?
Is my life worth nothing in the grand scheme of things?
Should I just give up altogether?
Life ends and begins with death.
Who says that I could become the legend that I want to be
if I were to continue living?
Would death be a better source?
I would die; People would forget about me;
no one would remember anything good nor bad about me,
so what is the point of living or dying if no one cares to
remember the truth?
And the truth is: nothing matters.
Life will continue on as if I were not in the picture at all,
and I would just be another innocent soul,
who fell short of their dreams.
I have no purpose in life.
I have no purpose in death.
I am nothing.

Chrystal Brockman
*Maricopa, AZ*

## Darkness Awaits

The darkness awaits
The lowly, the poor
The starving, the hungry
It will enter your door
Death will knock softly
Let him in, he will come
The death angel will stay
He only knows where your from
The darkness awaits
Your loved one, your love -
True love only stays awhile
Then darkness comes with a shove
The death awakens me
From my slumber, eternal rest
Life begs to stay - let her in
But no one is that blessed
The darkness awaits
A thief through the night
Be ready for thy storm
Bring back thy holy light

Hannah Mason
*Gilberts, IL*

## My Mask

Don't judge me, if you don't know me.
The mask is in the past.
It's to be filed with the rest, documented in memory,
Where truths and lies are separated,
And everything I've contemplated is lined up in a row.
They say brains is beauty,
But what if I don't got any?
What happens when nice isn't good enough?
Nice is my exterior.
I know I am inferior.
Now the cabinet's been reopened,
And there's paper everywhere.
I'm scrambling to clean it up,
To keep the cabinet closed,
Then I see him standing there leering down at me.
Paralyzed. Immobilized. Fear has come to play.
I hug the files to my chest and turn to him and say—
The mask is in the past!
And just like that he goes away.
I know he will come back someday,
But for now I file him away, in the back of my mind,
This time I lock it because my mask is in the past,
And that's where it will stay.

Ruby Bailey
*Kirkwood, MO*

## Nectar Rain

Sitting alone on a dim dreary night,
Facing an internal storm,
A single droplet fell from my cloud-filled eye,
The rain saccharine and warm.
A yellow tint this raindrop left,
Upon my colorless cheek,
For only bitter rain has ever fallen,
From clouds so dark and bleak.
Blossoming into a golden flower atop my briny flesh,
Creating a glowing, peaceful light nevertheless.
Down my arm the nectar climbed until reaching my vein,
My hazy blood it shall dissolve,
And furthermore obtain,
Spreading and expanding with no desire of pardon,
My single drop of nectar consumed the clouds,
And replaced them with a garden.

Elizabeth Condon
*Charles Town, WV*

## Waves

The waves crashing to the shore,
Like I've seen it all before.
The words spill out of my mouth,
Shivers rot down my spine.
The fear of death enters my mind,
Only till the wave goes back
Out far from the sand.
My eyes awaken once more,
And my cheeks ache from smiling.
If I can't control my feelings,
What is the point
I've treaded water my whole life.
But another wave is coming close,
I'll close my eyes again
And grab onto the hand of my long lost friend.

Nina Stoner
*Palatine, IL*

## A Lost Old Soul

My life has been a complete mess for some time,
I don't want to have these feelings on my mind.
All I have ever yearned for my entire life,
Is just a little peace love and happiness inside!
Inside my younger self and my adult self,
Why is it damn near impossible for me to receive help?
I didn't deserve to grow up lost,
Why, just why, can't I have the one thing in life that doesn't cost?
I grew up really hard, it's just so unfair,
Even now that I'm an adult, I just can't get there.
I'm not asking for fancy material things,
All I want is to give my children the ability to see,
the simplest things in life are free.
It's extremely exhausting to do,
To teach the things that were never taught to you.
Even more so, when you're a single mother of four,
Who has been knocked down so much, she just doesn't know what to do anymore
This world has been cruel to her since day one,
And is seeming to continue as the days come.
It is draining her trying to do it all,
With nobody to turn to, nobody to call.

Diana Quigley Patterson
*Nettleton, MS*

# Index of Poets

## D



## E



## F



## G



## H

## T



## U



## V



## W



## Y



## Z